PENGUIN BOOKS

SELLING MONEY

S. C. Gwynne was born in Worcester, Massachusetts, and was educated at Princeton and Johns Hopkins universities. He worked as an international loan officer for two major American banks during the foreign lending boom of the 1970s and early 1980s. He now lives in Los Angeles, where he is managing editor of *California Business,* the nation's largest business magazine.

SELLING MONEY

by

S. C. Gwynne

Penguin Books

PENGUIN BOOKS

Viking Penguin Inc., 40 West 23rd Street,
New York, New York 10010, U.S.A.
Penguin Books Ltd, 27 Wrights Lane, London W8 5TZ
(Publishing & Editorial) and Harmondsworth,
Middlesex, England (Distribution & Warehouse)
Penguin Books Australia Ltd, Ringwood,
Victoria, Australia
Penguin Books Canada Limited, 2801 John Street,
Markham, Ontario, Canada L3R 1B4
Penguin Books (N.Z.) Ltd, 182–190 Wairau Road,
Auckland 10, New Zealand

First published in the United States of America by
Weidenfeld & Nicolson 1986
Published in Penguin Books 1987

LIBRARY OF CONGRESS CATALOGING IN PUBLICATION DATA
Gwynne, S. C. (Samuel C.), 1953–
Selling money.
Reprint. Originally published: New York:
Weidenfeld & Nicolson, c1986.
Bibliography: p.
1. Loans, Foreign. 2. Loans, American. 3. Banks
and banking, International. 4. Banks and banking,
American. I. Title.
HG3891.5.G98 1987 336.3'435 87-6969
ISBN 0 14 01.0282 5

Printed in the United States of America by
R. R. Donnelley & Sons Company, Harrisonburg, Virginia
Set in Times Roman

To my mother and father

Contents

The bank system is, from the standpoint of formal organization, the most artificial and highly evolved product which capitalist society is capable of producing.

—KARL MARX

Time is the inflexible enemy of all false hypotheses.

—SAMUEL JOHNSON

SELLING
MONEY

Chapter One

WHISTLING PAST THE GRAVEYARD

1

You have probably never heard of Jesus Silva Herzog. His name belongs to the back pages of history, along with the names of others who unwittingly started panics or triggered disasters. Silva Herzog is merely a well-fed, upper-class Mexican technocrat, noteworthy only because on August 13, 1982, he was left holding the bag—the metaphor is apt—containing the financial and moral equivalent of an *$80-billion promissory note*, $26 billion of which was due and payable to the largest banks in the world. He himself had not borrowed all that money, but as the then-current finance minister of the Republic of Mexico he was obliged to pay it back.

In August 1982, Jesus Silva Herzog arrived on short notice at the U.S. Treasury Department in Washington and, in the words of a Treasury official, "turned his pockets inside out." He had tried desperately to keep up the fiction of Mexico's solvency during the summer months. Now he had exhausted all of his emergency lines of credit, and his own compatriots had managed to expatriate what remained of his hard-currency reserves. Mexico was bankrupt, an empty shell that had nothing to show for its unfathomably large debt. The purpose of Silva's humiliating pilgrimage was to reveal this horrible fact to U.S. monetary authorities. There was nothing else he could do.

While the rest of the world pursued its business, news of Mexico's insolvency spread quickly to fourteen hundred horrified creditor banks. *Eighty billion dollars.* It defied the imagination. Loans to Third World nations had barely even existed prior to 1970. Now a single country had been able to borrow a massive percentage of the capital and reserves of the world's largest banks. For over a decade, Mexico had been the darling of America's credit and capital markets. It had borrowed unprecedented amounts of money at rates usually reserved for Europeans and had been considered the shining example of why lending to developing countries was a sound and profitable practice. Now, Mexico suddenly stood out as incontrovertible proof that the banks had acted foolishly with billions of their depositors' dollars.

Within a week, Mexico exploded into headlines around the world. A crisis loomed: not since the 1930s had so much bank capital been threatened by such uncertain debt. But even more frightening than the size of the debt was the fact that the creditor banks were apparently ignorant of the state of Mexico's finances. The country had somehow gone bankrupt in secret, and the world's most powerful banks, which maintained full branches in the country, had not been privy to this. The idea was preposterous. Mexico had been in a near panic condition for months: an inflation rate of nearly 100 percent had played havoc with its currency; $100 million a day had been fleeing the country since the turn of the year; hundreds of thousands of upper-class Mexicans had been flooding the retail and real estate markets in Houston, Miami, and Los Angeles, desperately buying up dollar assets, knowing that the dollar would soon be revalued against the hopelessly weak peso. Mexico was being forced to repay the largest debt in history, at the most usurious rates in memory, in a currency that was rapidly depreciating. Yet the fact was that in the five months before Silva's visit, commercial banks had poured *$4 billion in new loans* into the country. And when this crisis exploded, the banks had no idea what Mexico had done with all that money. No one could explain exactly where it had gone.

Silva Herzog's visit was the high-water mark of a lending boom that had lasted a decade, representing the largest transfer of wealth from rich nations to poor nations in history. It also marked the beginning of the most profound international debt crisis ever, which by early 1983 included defaults by a dozen Third World countries and placed in jeopardy more than $300 billion—half the total debt of the developing world—in foreign loans.

From 1977 to the month that preceded Mexico's default in 1982, I was an international banker. For most of that time, I worked as a traveling loan officer for a $5-billion Ohio bank called the Cleveland Trust Company (later renamed AmeriTrust Company).*

It was perhaps the best time in history to be in the business of international banking, better than the Renaissance when Lorenzo the Magnificent through his Medici bank had financed the War of the Roses, better than the nineteenth century when the merchant banks of Baring, Rothschild, and Hambro had poured money into the United States and Latin America. There had never been such a large or sustained foreign lending boom, or so many foreign markets in which to operate, or so much money to dispense, or so few obstacles to its dispensation. And never had so many young men and women inherited an industry with such speed and lack of ceremony.

Before I reached my twenty-sixth birthday, after less than two years in the bank, I had been to twenty-five countries and was one of four bankers managing a $150-million international loan portfolio. It was an unusual life for a twenty-five-year-old. I traveled overseas three to four months a year. In Hong Kong, I was met at the airport by a chocolate-brown Rolls Royce, in the Philippines by a red Jaguar, in Saudi Arabia by a stretch Mercedes. I stayed at Claridges when in London, at the Oriental in Bangkok, and at the Meridien in Jeddah. I flew, ate, and drank first class and held two separate passports from the State Department to help me get safely in and out of the Middle East. I catalogue these items specifically to impress the reader, because this sort of corporate largesse is truly unusual, even in the world of international business. Such stylish travel is well beyond the financial reach of most people, even of most corporations. Yet in the late 1970s it was very much the perquisite of the young American banker, who was to be found in great numbers roaming the streets of Third World cities such as Kuala Lumpur, Rio de Janeiro, and Seoul, briefcase in hand, looking for deals to finance. He did not have to look far. Since OPEC had raised the

---

* Although Cleveland Trust changed its name to AmeriTrust in 1979, for the sake of clarity I have chosen to refer to it as The Cleveland Trust Co. throughout.

price of oil, both the public and private sectors of the Third World had been in a borrowing mood. In those years total loans outstanding to the non-OPEC Third World more than tripled—from $94 billion to $294 billion. And that is what paid for the bankers' epicurean comforts. The yearly increase in fees and interest income of America's top thirty banks had been spectacular.

I was part of a generation of young people who entered the banking business in the mid-1970s. It was the most conspicuous flowering of youth in business since the days of the bull markets on Wall Street a decade before. At the money center banks, international lending staffs both in the U.S. and abroad were rapidly doubling and tripling in size in the years following the first oil crisis. Even the Cleveland Trust Company, a conservative midwestern bank that had never had an international division to speak of, was staffing up: by 1975 it had a lending staff of twenty, two foreign exchange traders, and a support staff of forty, most of whom were under thirty years old. The same was true at regional banks across the country. We owed our jobs and our quick promotions to the size of the "surplus" the banking industry undertook to recycle. Some $600 billion would move from the haves to the have-nots within a decade. To do this, the banks had to create tens of thousands of jobs that had never existed before. They had to hire an army of people to find, negotiate, monitor, and collect that superabundance of foreign loans. The problem was that there were simply not enough experienced international bankers to go around by the time of the mid-1970s lending boom. Experience had to be accumulated quickly; what formerly took years now had to be compressed into months. Younger and younger people had to be promoted to positions of power. It was not a question of passing over older and more qualified people; they did not exist. The more loans the banks made, the faster middle management passed into the hands of the baby-boom generation, which was smart enough to know a good deal when it saw one.

It was wonderful to be young and upwardly mobile in the banking industry in those years. The stodgy old gentlemen's club of decades past had been dramatically transformed into one of the fastest and most competitive businesses on earth. Thousands of young people streamed in from colleges and business schools looking for that alluring combination of travel, glamour, foreign intrigue, and high-stakes international finance that modern banking seemed to offer. The profession became quite fashionable. Ivy League parties on New York's Upper East Side would be littered with international bankers. They were easy to spot. They were the ones telling the fascinating stories about bribery and corruption in Indonesia, or about how bauxite mines were built in Brazil. They were the world travelers, the cosmopolites who seemed to be so wise and experienced for their age, the ones who handled millions of dollars in foreign loans, who had met the finance minister of Venezuela or the chief of the Korean central bank.

It was even more wonderful to be so much in demand. Yet the demand had little to do with personal excellence and much to do with the banking industry's maniacal demands for personnel. There was frantic competition among banks for bankers with even a few years' experience. "Headhunters" stalked the international lending floors with annoying frequency. As a young loan officer I would typically receive five calls a month inquiring about my interest in various positions in banks around the country. It was a fast market, desperate enough that, with a well-considered move, you could double your salary and insure your vice-presidency before the age of thirty.

My career in banking coincided with the greatest boom cycle ever in international lending. I entered the banking industry just as the last few notions of sound overseas credit practice went sailing off into the blue yonder. I left the business a month before Jesus Silva Herzog's infamous visit to the U.S. Treasury. I can't say that I left because I had any foreknowledge of the coming crisis; I left because of the *dementia* of the system. There was something perverse about the job itself. I was called a loan officer, but I was no lender at all. I was nothing more than a conduit. I represented a bank that was supposedly lending the money. But then, as Karl Marx reminds us, the bank is not really the lender at all. The bank is just a middleman, a broker for the funds placed with it by individuals and corporations. I was not lending my own money, or even the money of a large, impersonal financial institution, but money that belonged to ordinary citizens who were collecting at best 5 percent interest on it, and who had unwittingly entrusted me with its disposition.

The practice of marketing foreign loans was even more illogical. "Selling" loans finally made no sense to me at all. In the years after the first oil crisis, how much convincing did it really take for Third World nations to borrow from foreign banks? They had been systematically drained of their international reserves, and they were desperate for foreign credit. My job was not to make a carefully considered credit decision, but to do exactly what American banks were trying to do at home with their retail operations; convince a prospective borrower that my bank's money was better than another's. This may seem a rather silly pursuit, but it was not silly to the banks. They devoted seemingly endless energy and resources to it. And it wasn't all just smoke, either: banks offered deposit services, cash management, funds clearance. and balance reporting services that made a difference to a borrower. But none of this changed the fact that I was "selling" loans, or the fact that the recycling of all that money was a political game from start to finish, since the leaders of the Third World had no choice but to borrow if they wanted to hold political power. The alternative was bankruptcy, default, and the sort of horribly unpopular austerity programs that later made the IMF infamous in the 1980s. Their predicament had been created by the highly political organization called OPEC; it would be assuaged by the banks with the cooperation of the political establishments of the industrial world. Given the premise that borrowers had infinite appetites, lending became a rather one-sided operation, with the flow of loans from specific banks to specific countries depending entirely on personal and institutional politics within the lending banks. It was this political process within the banks that turned sovereign credit on and off like water from a tap. When it was turned on, we loan officers were sent scurrying to the ends of the earth to drag up whatever business we could. When it was turned off, everything stopped. It made no difference finally who was selling those loans, or even who was running the people who sold them. They would be sold anyway. The banks' destiny was already contained in the original act: the raising of oil prices in 1973, which would be paid for by their international loans.

2

THERE WAS nothing special about August 13, 1982, in America, except that it was a Friday, which was unlucky, and that it was smack in the middle of one of the gloomiest times in recent memory. The American economy was in its deepest and most intractable recession since the 1930s. Except for two brief years of fragile, inflation-riddled prosperity in 1976 and 1977, Americans had seen nothing but hard times since the first oil crisis in 1973. The years 1974 and 1975 had been nightmarish: Americans waited in gas lines, paid five times what they had paid the year before for heat, and tried to remember how comfortable life had been a few years before. Then, just as the first shock had begun to abate, oil prices tripled again in 1978, which was followed by the worst sustained inflation of the century in the U.S. and a rise in interest rates that challenged the principal feature of the American dream: the ability to buy one's own home. The last truly prosperous time anyone could remember was 1972, the year Richard Nixon was reelected by the largest majority in American history. Inflation and interest rates continued to run high during the first half of 1982, and although economists were predicting recovery by the end of the year, no one believed it. The harsh decade had left its mark on the American psyche; the comfortable liberalism of the sixties had fallen on hard times.

Oddly enough, America's commercial banks had made more money during those hard years than ever before. The largest banks were making huge leaps in earnings, while the assets of individual banks began to approach $75 billion, $90 billion, even $100 billion. Anyone who cared to look would have seen the reason: more and more of America's banking assets consisted of foreign loans and investments. In some strange turnabout, America's banks seemed to be feeding off the global recession, turning hardship and political unrest into profits. The worse things got, the better the banks did. How could this be? By the summer of 1982, the answer was already appearing in print with alarming frequency under the rubric of the "debt crisis."

The numbers were staggering. In the decade since 1973, the developing world had borrowed $480 billion. By 1982 Latin America alone owed $300 billion to Western creditors. With the $120 billion borrowed before 1973, the total debt of the Third World had risen to $600 billion, of which $64 billion was held by the top nine American banks, amounting to 200 percent of their combined capital. The size of the debt was even more stunning when one considered that the source of these loans—the "Eurocurrency market"—did not even exist until the 1960s, and that there was no such thing as a commercial bank loan to a developing country prior to 1968. It had all happened in a flash, in the few years following the first oil crisis. And it explains how the banks were making all that money: At an interest rate of 15 percent per year, $600 billion generates a fair return.

To anyone who thought about the implications, this was an astonishing piece of news. It was not simply the absurd scale of the lending, but the whole process itself that was troubling. Americans were beginning to understand that many of these foreign loans had been funded with their own checking and savings accounts. Those who could grasp that also understood the fundamental change that had come over American banking in the latter half of the twentieth century: American money had become supranational, which meant that it had acquired a rapid and mischievous mobility, an ease of movement that made it dangerous. Suddenly $200 million of consumer deposits in, say, Minneapolis could be mobilized to fund an oil shipment to Morocco or Bolivia. The transaction would be perfectly characteristic of modern banking: clean, silent, electronic, and with little apparent regard for the borrower's capacity to pay back the loan at the end of its term.

Still to be explained, however, was *why* the banks had done this in the first place, when even the most casual observer could see that overseas lending was dangerous. One had only to look at the succession of minor debt crises in the late seventies and early eighties: Indonesia in 1975, Peru and Zaire in 1977, Turkey in 1978, Iran in 1979, and Poland in 1981. The banks seemed to have learned nothing from history. Ironically, it was not until after the panic in Iran in 1979 that they began what John Kenneth Galbraith called, with reference to 1929, "the mass escape into make-believe."

The reasons for the banks' "mass escape" were not clear, either within the financial community or outside of it, and the standard explanation of the crisis does not help. According to this explanation, the "debt crisis" is the result of the "expansionist" policies of "greedy" banks, "hungry" for profits, and untrammeled by laws or morals. This is deliberately misleading and grossly simplistic. Bankers are no greedier or less moral than anyone else. Besides, this explanation misses the point entirely, which is that the giant banks were merely the agents of much larger and less tangible economic forces unleashed by the quadrupling of oil prices in 1973. The essential point is this: the debt crisis is the flipside of the oil crisis—the invoice created by the world's sudden inability to pay for its energy.

That colossal quantity of money was not loaned to the Third World because the political climate suddenly favored it, or because the banks had just developed the specious argument that "sovereign nations cannot default." These were rearguard actions, adjustments by the banks and political establishments to a *fait accompli:* the draining of more than a trillion dollars from the economies of the non-OPEC world in the form of payments for crude oil and natural gas. The industrialized countries, though severely wounded by the price rise, could survive it. The Third

World could not. Thus between enriching itself and impoverishing the Third World, OPEC created the most dangerous economic disequilibrium in history: the unnaturally large surplus on OPEC's books became unnaturally large deficits on the books of the poor countries of the world. And that surplus had to move, or else the entire world financial establishment would come tumbling down with a crash not heard since 1929.

The surplus fell into the hands of the commercial banks: OPEC's panjandrums, who could buy only so many chateaux in Gstaad and condominiums in Palm Springs, placed almost all of their spare hundreds of billions on deposit with American and European banks in the 1970s. What the banks did with it was dictated by immediate political necessity. You could not just remove a trillion dollars from the world economy and continue merrily on your way. There was only one way to mitigate the potentially disastrous long-term effects of the oil price increase: recycle it back into the Third World where it could be used to buy Western exports. That the banks were suddenly able to lend massively abroad in the mid-1970s, with almost no interference from their governments, should surprise no one. The alternative to recycling was a deep, protracted, worldwide depression. And this was not a course political leaders would naturally choose to follow. A "let's take our lumps now" policy has never gotten anyone reelected. When assessing blame for the world debt crisis, the key is to remember that the political establishments of the First World could have regulated the banks' lending any time they chose to. The fact is that they did not.

It was a positively stirring, nearly surreal experience to watch Mexico boil up into a panic that August week in 1982, to watch the financial bureaucrats wrestle with their euphemisms while the premise of their whole system vanished in the polluted air of Mexico City. There could be no doubt about the implication of Mexico's default: the system, as conceived and executed by a legion of international bankers, did not work. In the five months that followed, some thirty countries would be forced to refinance more than $400 billion of foreign debt.

August 13, 1982, marks the end of the good old days of international banking: the end of the fast "volume" lending, the rate-cutting, the jumbo loans to foreign governments. Though it would not be the end of foreign lending by any means, from now on the game played by those eager young loan officers would be quite different. Now it would be a game of cut your losses, protect your flanks, and find ways to pretend to the regulatory agencies that your loan portfolios were not really in grave danger.

Technically, of course, the boom still had not gone bust. Mexico's crisis proved not that the system was going to collapse, only that it *could* collapse. No panic had occurred, there had been no runs on the banks, no social revolution had broken out in Mexico. Nothing had been destroyed but an assumption about the economic behavior of international debtors. But it was upon that assumption that the serene, fictitious world of my generation of bankers had been built. Now that it was gone a strange twilight had stolen over the system. There was nothing to do but to defer the reckoning, and pray that someone or something would intervene.

3

OF ALL of Mexico's creditors, the regional banks in the United States received the most severe shock that August. They were the lesser players of the international debt markets who had arrived too late to wield any power or influence, but just in time to get burned by the concatenation of foreign defaults, and then to be trapped in regulations that forced them to lend even more money to countries that had suspended payments. They were essentially the dilettantes of the foreign debt markets. They had been convinced by the big banks to join in on their huge loans. But they had never had any control to speak of: they had not originated most of the loans, they had not dictated terms, and were not in a position to manage them. As the events of the week of August 13 unfolded, the regional banks found themselves quite uncomfortably on the sidelines, watching a financial disaster which stood to cost them billions.

In the summer of 1982, it was not the regional banks but the large money center banks whose Mexican exposures became known: Citicorp, $3 billion; Bank of America, $2.7 billion; Chase Manhattan, $1.5 billion; Manufacturers Hanover, $1.9 billion; Morgan Guaranty, $1.2 billion; Chemical Bank, $1.4 billion. Theirs were the names one generally found in the news article typically headlined "World Debt Crisis Endangers Banks," giving the impression that these were the only banks with dangerous exposures in Mexico.

Although they dominate banking in the U.S., the top ten banks still constitute less than 25 percent of the system's assets. The next fifty banks down the ladder control $557 billion in assets, and viewed in aggregate they constitute a powerful presence in international banking. Most of them are regional banks in spirit if not in fact. They are banks such as Michigan National, Wachovia (North Carolina), Shawmut (Boston), Mercantile Texas, Maryland National, and First Alabama Bancshares. To illustrate their importance to the international debt market we need only take the example of Mexico, which in August 1982 owed approximately $48 billion to U.S. banks. Of that amount, the eleven largest U.S. banking companies held only $15.9 billion. The remaining $32.1 billion, or 67 percent of the total, was held by these smaller, regional banks.

One such regional bank was the Cleveland Trust Company. At the time I joined, it was the largest bank in the state of Ohio and the twenty-eighth-largest banking company in America. In the 1970s it became, along with many other regionals, an active lender to Mexico. And, like many other regionals, it found its Latin American portfolio in serious trouble in the early 1980s.

Cleveland is not the first place you would look for fast and loose international finance. It is not a town given to wild leaps of fantasy or emotion. Its most visible landmark is an area called the "Flats"—a mile-wide corridor on the near west side of town that follows the irregular looping of the Cuyahoga River. The Flats is a fantastic tangle of iron bridgework, steel mills, ore depots, chemical plants, and coal docks. In 1940 it held the second largest concentration of heavy industry in the world (after the Ruhr Valley in Germany). A monument to the industrialization of America, its history is instructive, since Cleveland was and is exactly what the landscape suggests: one of the great industrial machines of the twentieth century.

The wealthiest and most illustrious of Cleveland's banks was the Cleveland Trust Company. It was the quintessential midwestern industrial bank, both benefactor and beneficiary of Cleveland's industrial boom. It financed the businesses that built the Flats: iron ore, steel, shipping, salt, oil, chemicals, heavy equipment, machine tools, forge and foundry. It was the depository for the savings of a frugal and productive population of Eastern Europeans and the carrier of most of the mortgages in Cuyahoga County. The bank provided financing to build industrial empires in the heartland, and it became the final resting place for the profits of those empires. By 1977 it had accumulated 120 branches, $5 billion in assets, and $7 billion in trust funds under management. It was among the most powerful of America's fourteen thousand commercial banks, and held the city of Cleveland virtually in thrall. The sheer power of the bank was evident during the winter of 1977–1978, when a Cleveland Trust–led bank syndicate refused to refinance the city of Cleveland's notes after a disagreement with its mayor, precipitating a major financial crisis. The bank eventually relented, but only after the city had agreed to its terms. The bank was also the subject of many business legends in Cleveland. The Dow Chemical Company, for example, was said to have gotten its start in the back room of one of Cleveland Trust's branches.

Until the 1970s, Cleveland Trust was the paragon of the classical, inward-looking heartland bank. It drew its strength from the huge pool of profits and savings in Cuyahoga County and returned the money to the community in the form of retail and commercial loans. It became the prime intermediary of a small, heavily industrialized area in the Midwest. It did not need to look any farther than its own backyard for growth, stability, and financial success.

But in the early 1970s Cleveland Trust began an evolutionary cycle which would take it out of Cuyahoga County, out of Ohio, and ultimately out of the Western Hemisphere in search of new business. By 1982, Cleveland Trust had $1.5 billion in international commitments (largely undrawn lines of credit), and $700 million in outstanding foreign loans, $175 million of which were to Latin American countries. What was happening at Cleveland Trust was happening all over America. "Regional" banks were no longer what that quaint and obsolete term suggests. For the first time in history, the Cleveland Trust Company and banks like it were competing in the international marketplace, lending their depositors' money around the world.

All of this swam upstream against one of the strongest currents of isolationism in the country. The Midwest—particularly Ohio—is blessed by a superabundance of natural resources: coal, iron ore, more fresh water than anywhere else on earth, and productive farm and game lands. Its cities are among the most highly industrialized in the United States. With such surfeit—such self-sufficiency—isolationism is a predictable stance.

And yet out Cleveland Trust went into the great unknown in the early 1970s. It did so not because it was a liberal bank—it was one of the most conservative of America's top fifty banks—or because it was greedy for profits and willing to do anything to earn them. As we will see, the bank really had no choice in the matter.

Early on the morning of August 13, 1982, news broke on the Reuters wire that the Mexican government had closed its foreign exchange markets. It passed without notice in the Friday press, but on Cleveland Trust's international lending floor the bankers snapped to attention. The conventional wisdom is: you don't close an exchange market unless you've got a panic on your hands. Something was terribly wrong south of the border, but Cleveland Trust had no branches down there, no in-country personnel to advise it. The vice-president in charge of Mexico was summoned to the office of the senior vice-president in charge of the international division and asked what was going on. He answered that he didn't know. He was not alone. The New York banks were still worried about transferring money through the exchange markets; they had no inkling that the game was already up.

Without knowing it, Cleveland Trust and its fellow regionals were getting an object lesson in how a major sovereign nation went bankrupt. Mexico had been having its problems since the beginning of the year. A severe drop in world oil prices in 1981 had radically reduced its foreign exchange earnings. Inflation was running at well over 100 percent, and it was estimated that over a hundred million dollars a day in private capital had been fleeing the country since the turn of the year. The Mexicans had lost confidence in their own country's economy, and the smart money was getting out. By Thursday, August 12, the financial markets were in a full-scale panic, and the government had been forced to shut down all exchange markets. The idea was to prevent anyone from changing a peso to a dollar. What it meant was that Mexico did not have any more dollars to exchange. Between its debt repayment, its truncated oil earnings, and a panicked flight of capital, it had nearly exhausted its reserves.

On Wednesday, August 18, the story of Silva Herzog's visit to Washington got out: He had negotiated an emergency $2-billion credit, in the form of a $1-billion advance on oil sales and a $1-billion credit for grain imports. He had been in touch with the governments of France, Italy, Germany, Switzerland, and Japan pleading for similar relief. American banks still did not know how deep the crisis was. Even Citicorp, which held $3 billion in Mexican debt, did not know until Silva told them the next evening. On Friday, at an emergency creditors' meeting, Silva delivered his shocking request: Mexico wanted a ninety-day suspension on payment of all principal and interest on its debt.

Not until the Mexican exchange markets reopened, however, did Cleveland Trust realize the full hopelessness of its position. The bank had stuck sensibly to financing trade with the private sector and had a number of very good clients. But that week in August proved that it did not matter who your clients were. Country risk was country risk, and if the government of Mexico did not have the dollars to exchange for your client's pesos, then it did not matter how earnest or intrepid your client was. The phenomenal devaluation of the peso drove thousands of Mexican companies under and resulted in the loss of hundreds of millions of dollars by American investors. For Cleveland Trust, it meant that many of its loans would not be repaid, even though it had stuck to its conservative principles in its lending strategies. To make matters worse, it soon became apparent that the private sector was last in line for whatever favors the Mexican government was handing out.

That week in August 1982, the Cleveland Trust Company began a very long and painful odyssey. They would get used to it, used to the scare headlines and the predictions of doom, but they would never be quite at ease with those who asked the same question over and over again: How could the banks have lent that much money in the first place?

Chapter Two

INTO THE
MONEY VORTEX

I am about to embark upon a hazardous and technically unexplainable journey into the outer stratosphere.

—THE WIZARD OF OZ

1

IN THE winter of 1977–1978, through a whim of someone in personnel, I landed in the credit department of the Cleveland Trust Company. I was the rawest of financial novices, with a bachelor's degree in history, a master's degree from a graduate writing program, and two years' work experience teaching French in a private school. On the day I was hired, I could not distinguish an asset from a liability. I did not understand how a bank worked or what the employees of a bank, other than tellers, actually did. I was like most people, to whom banks are unnaturally powerful, vaguely frightening, and wholly mysterious. Because of my fluency in French, I was assigned to the international section of the credit department, the lowest rung on the international lending ladder. I could not have landed in a better place, even if I had known what I was doing. The prospects for advancement were extraordinary. International banking in the U.S. was exploding. It had already outstripped all forms of domestic banking and was, in fact, growing faster than any other major industry on earth. From 1964 to 1978, international bank lending had grown at an annual rate of 25 percent, compared to 5.25 percent for America's GNP and 7.5 percent for world trade. As financial figures grew, of course, so did the number of banking jobs. The absolute bulk of the money movements had created a sharp demand for a relatively new breed of young professional—the international loan officer. And the provenance of these people was the credit departments of the commercial banks, which were designed to feed the lending divisions continually with fresh talent. "Credit" was and is the straightest track to a job in international lending.

Cleveland Trust's international division was growing by leaps and bounds. Although this was not big-time international banking by any stretch of the imagination, half a billion dollars in loans and deposits had moved in the last seven years, and billions more had washed through the bank in the form of transfers, foreign exchange, and documentary credits. Here, the job track was blisteringly fast. In my first month at the bank, five of twenty-five analysts were promoted to lending positions after spending little more than a year in Credit. In all likelihood, they would be making million-dollar loans after only a year and a half with the bank. Banking was definitely not the stuffy old gentlemen's club I had feared it might be.

In the winter of 1978, I became part of a vast professional migration that was to have a profound effect on the world of international finance. It happened subtly, almost imperceptibly at first. Young men and women emerging from universities, intrigued by the romance of foreign affairs, began to join commercial banks in larger and larger numbers in the late 1960s and early 1970s. As more of them joined, and were swiftly promoted to positions of authority, the better the jobs looked. Like most banking trends in the last thirty years, this one started at the large banks in New York, Chicago, and California and spread from there to regional banks across the country. By 1970, the top fifteen U.S. banks already employed thousands of international bankers who traveled the world, cut deals on foreign soil, and lived in high style. Banks like Citicorp, Bank of America, Chase Manhattan, and Continental Illinois possessed worldwide branch networks where they employed a mixture of Americans and locals. In the 1970s, America's regional banks followed these big banks overseas, cautiously at first, using select officers to scout the market and establish banking relationships; later they would set up their own "rep" offices and branches in London, Nassau, Luxembourg, Tokyo, Singapore, or Hong Kong. "Going global" was the wave of the early seventies, and while for the big banks like Citicorp (which had been global for some sixty years) this was simply more of the same, for the regionals it was a radical departure from the old ways. By the mid-1970s, banks all over the provincial United States—in cities like Minneapolis, Cleveland, Atlanta, Houston, St. Louis, New Orleans, Detroit—were staffing up their credit departments and international lending divisions to meet the new demand.

A whole new set of rules governed the careers of these young bankers, which often put them at odds with older bankers who had come up through a long, slow system of rewards and punishments. Promotion of young bank officers was so swift that the notion of "deferred gratification" had gone completely out of vogue. As with pilots in wartime, there was no time for seasoning, no time to allow untried youngsters to sit back and absorb experience over a period of years. The need for professional money-movers was immediate and insatiable.

International banking was more than just a new type of job—it was a *phenomenon*. The exotic and previously little-known term "wholesale banking" was suddenly on the lips of fresh-faced college seniors across the country. Wholesale banking refers to that part of a commercial bank that lends to and takes deposits from large companies. It is not to be confused with branch or "retail" banking, which deals with small companies and ordinary people like you and me, and from which, as Anthony Sampson put it, it is "as remote as the moon." The wholesale or "corporate" bank is the part of the bank that most people do not see, do not understand, and therefore generally do not trust.

Wholesale banking was the new craze in American finance in the 1970s, the result of the legislative strangulation of the commercial banks' retail operations. Throughout most of this century, America's banks grew by expanding their *retail* divisions—that is, their branches where they took deposits from people and made mortgage, consumer, and small-business loans. Corporate banking existed, of course, but it was limited. Banks in the U.S. did not make loans to business at terms longer than one year until after World War II. As the banks grew, however, they began to bump up against state laws prohibiting their expansion. It happened in almost every state: the retail operations of the big banks in New York were confined to Manhattan Island; in Chicago, a "unit banking" law permitted a bank to have only a single branch; in Cleveland, Cleveland Trust was legally bottled up inside Cuyahoga County. In order to keep growing, commercial banks began to look to the wholesale bank, and eventually to the international wholesale bank, for loans and deposits. And thus a dynamic new industry was born in the 1950s and 1960s. By the 1970s worldwide corporate lending would evolve into one of the slickest, most competitive of businesses, as the top banks fought for the accounts of large, successful companies, and began to expand quickly across state and national boundaries.

With the rise of the corporate, wholesale bank came a new type of person, quite unlike the bankers of old who were reconciled to conservative business practices, low pay, and a long climb to the top of the ladder. Corporate bankers were utterly different from the retail bankers: the retail banker was a soft-spoken, reassuringly dull gentleman in a light-brown polyester suit and laceless shoes to whom you applied for an auto loan. A corporate banker was by design a much more impressive creature. He was generally turned out in a $350 pinstripe suit, a blue, button-down Brooks Brothers oxford shirt, $125 wing-tip brogans, and he looked, or tried to look, like he had gone to boarding school somewhere. A corporate banker was a salesperson, a pusher of products. The corporate banker was the one who roamed the world in 1978 peddling loans in Morocco and Korea; he was the one having cocktails with the Argentine finance minister or flying to Singapore for an emergency loan meeting. By contrast, the retail banker was a thoroughly local character. He did not go anywhere, nor did he sell anything. He acted mainly as a screen to make sure that bad loans did not slip through the bank's credit networks.

I had entered the corporate world and would ever after be expected to look and behave as though I belonged there. And so I—and thousands of others—went rushing off to purchase expensive suits and shoes and overcoats, even though the financial strain caused by such purchases was nearly unbearable on a salary of $10,000 a year. Once I looked like a banker, I had only to worry about learning to think like one, and I was astonished at how easy this was.

"You cannot make a man by standing a sheep on its hind legs," wrote Max Beerbohm. "But by standing a flock of sheep in that position you can make a crowd of men." He might have been describing the process of social and professional assimilation at a commercial bank. I was poorly qualified to become a banker. But I soon learned that nearly everyone else was too, and that banks had operated this way for a long time. The "sheep principle," in essence, is that in a social group you can make out of men and women whatever you want to. The practice of hiring and promoting financial innocents was an old tradition of the banking business. Banks, more than any other type of corporation, preferred to train their own, to introduce them to their trade secrets without interference from business schools and other outsiders. It was for this reason that, as foreign debt rose to ever more dangerous levels, so many bankers seemed unable to see beyond their own noses. Banking was one of the last industries to hold the view that MBAs were spoiled rich kids, bounty jumpers who could not be trusted to remain past their first promotions. And Cleveland Trust was one of the last big banks to relinquish that view. "Those MBAs are terrific at making loans," the wry old bankers on the credit committees would say. "It's only when they have to *collect* them that they run into trouble." At the entry level, commercial banks preferred ignorance to savvy, enthusiasm to polish. This was all in my favor: My lack of a business degree was suddenly transformed into a virtue; I would be trained to look, think, and act like a banker; and I would be taught their peculiar, clubby view of the world.

The job of the international credit analyst was to study the creditworthiness of a variety of phenomena. At the bottom of every big international export deal or term loan was a large pile of numbers compiled by credit analysts. The numbers told the senior vice-presidents on the loan committees how strong the borrower was, how much the borrower could pay back, how many of the borrower's assets could be liquidated quickly to pay off a loan, and what the political and economic climate was in the borrower's country. It was remarkable how easily everything reduced to numbers: economic stability as a ratio of exports to debt service; political volatility as measured by per capita income or an inflation index. All these numbers had to be spread, tallied, and made sense of, and that was my entry-level job at Cleveland Trust.

I arrived smack in the middle of the great, golden age of international lending, at a bank that in 1978 found itself in the outer eddies of a one-trillion-dollar money vortex. Cleveland Trust was expanding quickly, competing with thousands of other commercial banks for a piece of the forty billion dollars that would be loaned from the banks to the rest of the world in 1978. To understand the slippery logic which had allowed it to become so deeply involved is to understand the allure of the system itself. Cleveland Trust in 1978 was a microcosm of the new world of international finance.

2

THE INTERNATIONAL division occupies the ninth floor of the Cleveland
Trust Tower, a modern twenty-six-story building on the corner of East
Ninth Street and Euclid Avenue, in a small neighborhood of skyscrapers. To the north it faces the blue waters of Lake Erie, stretching clear
to the horizon. To the west and south is the gloomy accretion of smoke,
soot, and heavy industry of the Flats, where Cleveland Trust has been
making loans and picking up deposits since 1895. At sunrise on a winter
day you can watch from the tower as the sun rises behind the billowing
smoke and blast furnaces of Republic Steel, one of the largest steel
companies in America and one of the bank's clients in good standing.
"Where there's smoke, there's money," J. D. Rockefeller, a Cleve-
lander who built his first oil refinery in the Flats, was supposed to have
said. There was in fact a good deal of money left in Cleveland in 1978—
it was the country's third largest corporate headquarters for Fortune 500
companies that year—and the lion's share of it was safely locked away
at the Cleveland Trust Company.

Next to the tower is a huge, neoclassical domed structure called the
Rotunda, an historic landmark which houses Cleveland Trust's show-
case branch. The tower is impressive, a Marcel Breuer design with vaulted
granite entrance halls and sculpted exterior walls. But it pales beside the
Rotunda, which is a more precise symbol of the bank's historic power
and influence. Inside, the Rotunda is all marble and brass. There is a
strange, unnatural silence—the sort of silence that prevails when people
come into the presence of great wealth and power. The Rotunda is the
architectural jewel of a street that at the turn of the century housed more
millionaires than Fifth Avenue in New York. Their magnificent homes
are gone now, but the Rotunda still keeps many of their fortunes. It is
the retail bank par excellence, where even a rich man can feel a certain
thrill as his money is handed to him across that ancient stone counter.

Its elegance notwithstanding, the Rotunda was still a retail bank. In
1978 the real action was next door in the tower, which housed the corporate bank. I spent that year of lonely apprenticeship in a ghastly orange module in the credit department. The credit department had no real
existence of its own, but operated as a support area and farm club for
the various divisions of the corporate bank: national, metropolitan, real
estate, leasing, and international. Because I spoke French I had been
assigned to the international division, even though this involved analyz-

ing statements in Spanish, a language I had never studied or spoken. That discrepancy apparently did not bother anyone, so I blundered ahead. Thus began my time in the international division where, for the first time, I was able to observe the system at work. It offered an astounding look, after a mere month or so at the bank, into the incandescent heart of the financial machine that would pump $40 billion into the Third World that year. It also provided contact with an even more interesting phenomenon: the bank officers of the international division who actually made those foreign loans.

These officers were engaged in a business that the bank's august founders would never have dreamed of: a foreign sales operation. The division's young account officers were conduits for hundreds of millions of dollars that had left Cuyahoga County in the form of foreign debt. They were the real salespeople of the international debt market, operatives who traveled 50,000 miles or more a year to sell local checking and savings accounts in places as remote as Brazil, Korea, and Abu Dhabi. Most of their job descriptions had not existed at Cleveland Trust five years before.

Their habitat on the ninth floor had none of the Rotunda's ponderous elegance. Instead it had the deliberately clean, antiseptic look of the new corporate bank, a look that (like the modular space of the credit department) was duplicated in nearly every major bank in the country. The large, open area occupied by the account officers was known as the "loan platform." This was a curious choice of words, for there was nothing about the ninth floor to suggest a platform, except that it was flat. I never discovered the origin of the phrase, but I assumed that the banks had borrowed the term from industry, as though to suggest that some sort of tangible product was being handled there (as in "drilling platform'" or "loading platform"). In fact, the "product" of Cleveland Trust's international division was visible nowhere on the premises. There were no teller windows, no hands furiously peeling off cash, no safe deposit boxes, no vaults containing cash and securities. It was, in effect, an *invisible* bank that held invisible assets of more than half a billion dollars. Loan disbursements and remittances moved silently, electronically, and in large increments by means of telecom machines in the back rooms. Cash was something that the international bank officers carried in their pockets to buy lunch or cigarettes with; professionally, the money they used consisted of electronic blips in the ledger of the banking system.

The ninth floor was comfortable and quiet; a nice place to work. The loan platform was the front room of two large, open rooms. The main furnishings were desks, and the general configuration was reminiscent of a secretarial pool or a clerical "bullpen." But there the similarity stopped. On the walls hung original paintings by Lichtenstein, Calder, Piranesi, and Stella. The carpet was deep, plush; the desks were mahogany, with high-backed leather armchairs. There were only two private offices on the floor. They contained a senior vice-president, head of the division, and a high-ranking vice-president, his deputy manager.

The lack of walls or offices on the ninth floor was part of a national banking tradition. Apparently there was originally a good reason for it. In the old, single-room bank, it was considered both unseemly and suspicious for the teller (the man who handled the money) to be found behind closed doors with the accountant (the man who kept track of the money). Without walls, the two would always be visible to the bank's clientele, which imparted a sense of propriety to the whole operation. That, at any rate, was the traditional reason that the bank's PR folks offered. And while there is some truth in it, it is perhaps a shade truer to say that nowadays the setup reflects more the phenomenon of "title inflation," which has crammed the banks so full of senior vice-presidents, vice-presidents, and assistant vice-presidents that they could not possibly all be given private offices. By the mid-1970s, title inflation had reached an almost humorous level at American commercial banks, and you had to be able to decode the titles themselves to find a banker's true level of responsibility. If you were not an assistant vice-president by the age of thirty, there was something wrong with you. If you had not made vice-president by the time you turned thirty-four, then you'd better start looking for another career. In an average nonbank corporation, there are usually only two or three vice-presidents, who account for the various broad divisions of the company: sales, operations, finance, and so on. In the modern commercial bank, there are dozens of vice-presidents *within each division*, which means that they are really nothing more than lower- or middle-level managers. What accounted for title inflation, especially in the corporate bank, was simple psychology. When you were handling millions of loan and deposit dollars for a client, the client naturally felt better about it if you had a title. This increased the client's sense of his own importance and measurably increased his confidence in the account officer. Plus the title neatly justified letting thirty-year-olds play with that amount of money in the first place.

To an outsider, the activity on the ninth floor was incomprehensible. It was impossible to guess what was going on behind that even, permanent hum of solicitation that came from the loan platform: men and women speaking into telephones, hanging up, pondering, redialing, changing languages in midstream perhaps, or raising their voices to accommodate a bad connection to Prague or Santiago. The international bank really was invisible, even to the insiders. Though it had a material existence on the ninth floor, it was really an aggregation of immaterial human and corporate relationships. These relationships were sustained by the least tangible of all the things floating around the international bank—*credit*—and their fruits were impalpable movements of electronic units of value: loans, deposits, and foreign exchange. By design, the business was such that it had to be slowly and thoughtfully described to the apprentice, as the apprentice worked through each of the complex relationships.

By the winter of 1978, Cleveland Trust had a staff of seventeen international "calling" officers—a designation that distinguished the loan peddlers from the sedentary types who handled the nuts and bolts of international banking operations. Collectively, they traveled fifty-one months a year, made some four thousand individual sales calls on clients, and covered seventy countries on every continent in the world. With the corporate solipsism that was typical of the time, the bank had carved the world up into five areas of responsibility, each governed by a satrap who bore the title of vice-president, none of whom was older than thirty-five. The areas represented were Western and Eastern Europe; the Middle East and Africa; Asia and the Pacific; Latin America; and the U.S. and Canada for export finance.

The satraps sat along the western wall of the ninth floor, a quiet, genteel zone that looked through enormous plate-glass windows onto East Ninth Street and the frozen heart of the city. From the windows you could watch snow dart crazily before the buildings, caught in the vortices of wind that came off the icebound lake. The most successful among them—and the most representative of this new generation of bankers who had been handed the world on a filigreed platter—was Charles Hammel, a thirty-one-year-old graduate of the prestigious Fletcher School of Law and Diplomacy. He ran the bank's lending operations in an area of the world roughly comprising the fullest reaches of the Moslem and Ottoman empires, and to cover this domain he traveled at least 100,000 miles a year. He was among the first people hired into the international division, and his own story is the story of international banking at Cleveland Trust. Starting from scratch, Hammel and a few others created a large loan portfolio and established a formidable presence in the world financial community. Hammel wrote many of the rules by which the bank conducted foreign business. He was bright, young, and above all he had entered the bank at a time when power, privilege, and responsibility had been his for the asking.

For those with fantasies of travel and adventure, Hammel's job seemed like a dream. As a banker, he was the lineal descendant of Lorenzo the Magnificent, the fifteenth-century Medici banker who lent money to the monarchs of Europe through branches all across Europe. Lorenzo was the pope's banker, the most famous patron of the Renaissance, and was the prototype of the refined, gentlemanly, and aggressive international bankers who would come to populate the twentieth century. The business had always been risky and glamorous, and in Hammel's era it was no different. International bankers still took chances in places with unpronounceable names, and they still commanded the attention of foreign kings and princes.

Hammel traveled three to four months a year overseas, as often in Paris, Geneva, and Luxembourg as in Algiers, Kuwait City, and Casablanca. Cleveland Trust, of course, paid for his travel and also paid for all of his business entertainment, which was considerable. In a few months he traveled more than most people did in a lifetime. His memory was crammed with enough minutiae and oddball stories to fill a Joseph Conrad novel. For those who went backpacking around Europe in their early twenties, then somewhat reluctantly chose more sedentary, practical careers, Hammel seemed to have found the perfect profession. He had it both ways: travel to exotic places, adventure, money, and ultimately, at the end of each voyage, safety.

His job was to sell loans, door to door, in the Third World. If that seems like a strange idea, then its practice will seem stranger still. On a typical four-week trip to peddle his wares in the Middle East and North Africa, he would knock on one hundred and twenty doors. He did exactly what a traveling salesman does in Gary, Indiana. He flew in, checked into a hotel, got up the next morning and made his sales calls, then flew out the next night. He had some notable successes.

Because of Hammel, Cleveland Trust was the fourth largest foreign bank, by outstanding loans, in Israel. Thanks to Hammel's relationship with a displaced Iraqi trader, Cleveland Trust had financed the sale of most of the air-conditioners in Kuwait. He financed steel mills in Algeria and refrigerators in Saudi Arabia. Thus far his track record was flawless: he had not lost the bank a dime.

How much he actually made for the bank was harder to say. The cost of his upkeep was huge. He flew first class and stayed at five-star hotels. He entertained at the best restaurants in the world. A four-week trip might cost the bank as much as $20,000 and Hammel made three or four of them a year. Add to this his domestic travel, salary, and perks, and it came to something like $140,000 a year just to keep him on the road. How did he earn his keep? Consider an example from one of his trips: On a visit to Israel, Hammel convinced the largest Israeli bank— Bank Leumi—to borrow a $20-million banker's acceptance (a type of short-term loan), and he executed the deal upon his return home. At a 1 percent spread, net, for six months, Cleveland Trust made $100,000 pure profit. Hammel had covered over 70 percent of the cost of his upkeep with *just one deal*. His total portfolio ran to something like $75 million. At an average 1 percent spread over cost of funds, the bank would earn $1,125,000. Those profits of course did not include the money earned from the deposits placed with Cleveland Trust by Hammel's clients, which represented free, lendable money to the bank. Against these numbers, Hammel's $140,000 seemed insignificant, a fact of which Hammel was well aware, and which contributed to the sort of expense-account arrogance common to bankers in the 1970s. Such personnel/profits multiples were common in international banking, explaining in part why the international banks were turning such huge profits: One man, given a liberal credit policy and a generous expense account, could rake in millions.

Hammel epitomized the new breed, the avant-garde of banking in the 1970s. He was happy, industrious, and making a good living. What he was doing made sense to him. It was neither his job nor his desire to worry about large, unwieldy abstractions, such as whether what he did was threatening the stability of the world financial system. These questions came later, after the catastrophe of 1982. In 1978 the most curious aspect about Charles Hammel was the incredible speed of his—and Cleveland Trust's—rise to prominence in international banking. After all, his job did not even exist at the bank before 1972. Why, suddenly and with no precedent, had this peculiar phenomenon occurred? Why did the international division exist at all? Why were bankers out there in those unusual places, selling money in foreign countries whose governments were often hostile to our own? What could possibly have led them to believe that it would be a sound idea to dispatch Charles Hammel overseas to lend such a large quantity of American money?

3

THE FIRST thing to understand about Cleveland Trust is that it never wanted to be an international bank. Unlike some of its more aggressive counterparts in the rest of the world, it eschewed, and indeed feared, any financial business outside of the continental limits. It was a traditional, conservative heartland bank. The last thing it needed or wanted was to worry about the fate of its depositors' money in Morocco, Indonesia, or Venezuela.

But Cleveland Trust never really had a choice. It was the victim, then the beneficiary, and then the victim again of forces much greater than itself that revolutionized the banking industry in America at mid-century. What caused Cleveland Trust and other regional banks to go international in the first place was *history,* the great sweep of an invisible hand. To understand this, we must first examine what happened to the domestic banking industry in general—and to Cleveland Trust in particular—after World War II. The "revolution" in banking that everyone talked about—in electronics, automated tellers, credit cards, and the sale of new services such as "cash management"—wrought undeniably significant changes, but it had more to do with refining existing business than with exploring uncharted territory. The *real* banking revolution occurred within the corporate bank, and was chiefly the result of a conflict between two powerful forces. The first was the law, which sought to restrict banks' retail operations. The second was the banks' desire for infinite growth. Together the clash resulted in the rise of corporate banking on a national scale, and corporate banking eventually landed the banks on foreign shores.

The Cleveland Trust Company began its corporate existence in 1895. By 1920, its deposits had passed the $100-million mark, and it counted one quarter of Ohio's population as its depositors. Its clients included Sears & Roebuck, Firestone, Armour, General Motors, and General

Electric. The bank emerged from World War II as one of the nation's most powerful banks; in 1945 its assets exceeded $1 billion. (No U.S. bank prior to 1926 had had assets of $1 billion.) By 1966 it had seventy-eight branches with assets over the $2-billion mark; that year it ranked as the twentieth largest bank in America.

All of this had been achieved in spite of stringent, overbearing financial regulation. Since its inception, Cleveland Trust's branch operations had been restricted to a single county. The regulation was part of the quirky landscape of American banking, which had long been conditioned by America's fear of the power of large financial institutions. Unlike Europe, where banking power had long been concentrated in the hands of elite groups, the U.S. in the 1830s, had established what it called "free banking," when Jacksonian democrats crushed the second Bank of the United States. The result of the bank crisis of the 1830s was an extremely liberal chartering policy: Anybody could start a bank, and just about anybody did, as the country pushed westward in the nineteenth century. So liberal were the bank chartering policies that in 1921 there were an incredible 30,456 registered commercial banks in the United States. As a result of this rapid breeding, a debate arose in the early twentieth century over the right of banks to branch. Between 1919 and 1929 over a dozen states passed legislation restricting the growth of individual banks, in a spirit reminiscent of the 1830s. The primordial fear was still intact.

But it was the Glass-Steagall Act of 1933 that more than anything else determined the structure of American banking for the rest of the twentieth century. Glass-Steagall was occasioned by the worst banking disaster in history—more than nine thousand banks failed between 1929 and 1933—and it contributed even more than the stock crash to the severe recession of the 1930s. The act not only created the Federal Deposit Insurance Corporation, it also prohibited interstate branch banking and left intrastate branching regulation up to the state governments. This resulted in the bewildering array of banking laws that now exists in this country. One third of the states prohibit or severely limit bank branching; another one third permit branching only within restricted areas (city, county); and the remaining one third permit banks to operate anywhere in the state.

Ohio's law restricted the branching of banks to their home counties. This law was liberalized in the 1970s to allow for multibank holding companies, and later to allow de facto statewide branching. But for almost the whole of its existence, the bank had been trapped within the boundaries of Cuyahoga County, the half-moon-shaped strip of land on the southern shore of Lake Erie that contained the city of Cleveland. The effect of such a law is obvious: Cleveland Trust would grow to a certain size, and then grow no more. Its profits would eventually stagnate, then decline, as it competed with other banks for market share in a static population base. In Cuyahoga County there was an additional problem: the population was actually declining because of the southward migration in the 1970s that came to be known as the "Sunbelt Exodus." Cleveland Trust found itself locked into a single county with four major and a host of minor competitors. It was facing a textbook case of diminishing returns. This was simply unacceptable to the bank which, like everyone else in America in the latter half of the century, had decided that *growth* was the sine qua non of success in the modern business world.

But while the law restricted retail operations, it had much less to say about how a bank must deal with its corporate clients. Cleveland Trust had always been a corporate bank, to the degree that it provided short-term credit to the large local companies (Republic Steel, Eaton, TRW, Sherwin Williams) and to local factories of corporations based elsewhere (General Electric, General Motors). As retail banking began to look more and more finite, the bank made a wonderful discovery. There were no laws against making a loan to a company in another state, nor were there any restrictions on taking that company's deposits, provided the deposits were housed in Cleveland. Cleveland Trust quickly discovered that its desire for growth could be satisfied by the large number of companies in the United States—outside of Ohio—with whom it could deal freely. The law, then, defined the new markets into which the bank could venture, effectively pushing it forever out of Cuyahoga County. The result was the invention of the all-new, nonpublic domain of corporate banking.

Banking had changed. It was no longer a system which operated within towns, cities, or single counties. Your deposit in the local branch was no longer being used to finance your neighbor's mortgage. It had suddenly become part of the funding for a leasing deal to a company in Florida, or a line of credit to a factory in Oklahoma. The money was suddenly quite mobile, in a way that would have been regarded as heretical before World War II. It had become part of a multifarious pool of funds which the bank no longer earmarked for a specific destination.

While the banks continued to pretend that they believed in the sanctity of their particular local communities, they were already behaving as though there was only one big community—America itself. "Intermediation"—the process of taking deposits and making loans—would no longer be confined within a neighborhood, a small town, or even a city, but would extend across thousands of miles. It would be a national, rather than local, system. This was pure, profit-oriented bank pragmatism, but it went against what many Americans believed was a fundamental moral principle: they did not trust money that traveled long distances to borrowers who were unknown to them. They could not change it, of course. The good old days were long gone.

In 1972, the year it became a true international bank, and the year Charles Hammel began his travels overseas, Cleveland Trust was one of the strongest, most profitable banks in America. It was the largest bank in the state of Ohio. It had become a big-league corporate bank, with a staff of thirty-five wholesale loan officers who canvassed the United States from coast to coast. With such a rich, secure position in the banking industry, why did Cleveland Trust feel the need to "go global?"

It was a curious circumstance, especially for a bank that had always been something of a nervous Nellie when it came to business outside of the continental limits. "The trouble with foreign affairs," said Lord Rawnsley, "is that they attract foreigners," a statement with which Cleveland Trust's management would have agreed. Its board of directors and upper management felt ill at ease with foreign business, which they regarded as volatile, risky, and above all something that they could not understand. It was enough to send officers to Alabama, they thought, with its peculiar laws and ways of doing business. Why on earth would you want to lend money in a place like Latin America, where they overthrew their leaders every few months? Why try to make the world behave like a small community?

The reason was disarmingly simple: by the 1970s, 20 percent of American goods and services were sold overseas. One out of every five jobs in the U.S. was created by foreign sales. As a big-league corporate bank, Cleveland Trust had big-league corporate clients, and most of these clients had significant overseas operations. Whatever Cleveland Trust management's conservative, isolationist opinions might have been, they were suddenly confronting a new, and to many of them horrifying, problem: their clients not only needed but expected the bank to finance their international trade. To the corporations it was perfectly logical. They had clients or subsidiaries in, say, Taiwan who needed their products. But the foreign entity needed to borrow money to finance the purchase, as most companies would. This was a conventional form of "buyer finance" and Cleveland Trust had done it thousands of times in the U.S. If the Taiwanese buyer was creditworthy, then why should the bank not make the loan?

Cleveland Trust could politely refuse, of course, saying that it did not trust foreigners with good, clean American money. But the result of such a policy was clear. In the frantically competitive environment of modern corporate banking, either Cleveland Trust "followed" the client or it lost the business. It was this above all that made Cleveland Trust an international bank and necessitated Charles Hammel's overseas solicitations. To ignore the internationalization of its clients' trade would weaken it immeasurably in precisely the area it had targeted as its prime money-maker: domestic corporate banking. In that respect, it did not really have a choice in the matter. It could limit its international operations to a select few, but it could not forestall the trend. It had to go global, and the only question was, How far? When Cleveland Trust made its definitive leap into international banking, it found that it was not so bad out there as it had thought, that foreigners could be trusted after all. To its pleasant surprise, it also found that it could make a great deal of money overseas, and, even better, that a new part of the bank had been freed from the old retail restrictions on growth.

Charles Hammel, then, was the product of a long trend that began with the internationalization of American commerce after World War II. Cleveland Trust had been a latecomer to the international scene. The money center banks were already moving aggressively in the 1960s in offshore markets to avoid restrictive measures.

But in the 1970s Cleveland Trust moved to close the gap, and Hammel was among the first enlisted to accomplish that. He had come of age at exactly the right moment. He would make loan officer in his mid-twenties, assistant vice-president in his late twenties, vice-president when he was thirty-two, and head of the division at thirty-six. His career rise was being duplicated in banks all across the country, most of which were subject to the same international pressure, and which followed, in one form or another, a similar path to foreign shores.

By 1978, Cleveland Trust had a loan portfolio of $550 million, a 17.5 percent equity in an Israeli-British bank, and a Nassau branch to handle its Eurodollar loans. It was making money hand-over-fist in an extremely optimistic lending market. It had moved solidly into the second tier of American international banks and was operating in the fast, sophisticated Eurocurrency and foreign exchange markets. It had already gone well beyond its initial desire to cover its domestic client base. In 1978 it was preparing to go even further out into the wild blue yonder of international lending.

Chapter Three

"THE PARADISE OF LITTLE FAT MEN"

1

IN THE credit department of the Cleveland Trust Company, I encountered the perverse logic of the international banking system at its most elemental level. Credit was the fiber that bound the system together, forming the intricate web of truth, half-truth, hearsay, gossip, falsehood, and outright deceit that justified the manic lending spree of the 1970s and early 1980s. On its own terms, the logic of credit made perfect sense— each incorrect postulate led in a reasonable, orderly way to each false axiom. By the late 1970s, the international commercial banks had worked out "country risk analysis" systems with the zeal and precision of the Council of Nicaea defining the doctrine of the Holy Trinity. The more they lent, the more they justified it with their new mathematical "econometric" models. The crises that followed August 1982 showed how radically wrong they had been, how their elaborate credit systems had failed utterly to protect the interests of their depositors and stockholders. It was only then that some bankers were moved to admit that their risk analysis had been little more than sophistry and mumbo-jumbo—or, as some critics had it, a pack of lies.

As a credit analyst, I processed the "hard" information that supported the bank's foreign loans. I wrote "country studies" which examined political and economic risk; I analyzed the financial statements of foreign banks and corporations; I ran credit investigations on prospective borrowers. Within a few months I became proficient at delivering what was expected of me. At the same time I realized not only how soft this hard information was, but also that I was just a bit player in a perverse, global confidence game, its hair-splitting systematization of the financial universe resting upon a single false premise: that commercial banks could predict with reasonable accuracy the course of history. The concept seems ridiculous, and yet it was the linchpin of the entire system of international credit. The large commercial banks in the U.S. used it to justify the loaning of billions of dollars—not to mention huge percentages of their capital—to volatile, underdeveloped countries at terms often exceeding seven years. I learned very soon that questions about the fundamental soundness of the system's logic were anathema; it was like challenging the existence of God at a fundamentalist church meeting. The point was to play by the rules, because that was how the bank made money. Besides, the rules had been operating for a long time, and no one had lost any big money yet.

This was the first and most striking absurdity of the international lending business. The banks behaved, as the *Institutional Investor*'s Darrell Delamaide put it, "as though their brave new world of sovereign lending were exempt from history." The systematic optimism that made this possible calls to mind Dr. Pangloss in Voltaire's satire, *Candide*. The international banks had, like Dr. Pangloss, remained tireless optimists, choosing to ignore all of the evidence of hardship and impending disaster. In the 1970s, the evidence had been plentiful. Indonesia, Zaire, Peru, Chile, and Turkey had all been considered good risks. They had borrowed heavily and then, to the banks' horrified surprise, quickly ran out of foreign exchange and no longer had the ability to service foreign debt. The amounts involved were small compared to the gargantuan sums involved in the defaults of the 1980s. Still the lesson should have been learned: Even in the short run, "country risk analysis" was pure hogwash. Remarkably, the banks would go on to endure the violent revolt in Iran in 1979 and the bona fide bankruptcy of Poland in 1981—both of which they had completely failed to predict—without losing faith in their ability to augur world political and economic history. Up to the very minute of Mexico's default in 1982, they had been busily arranging loans, confident that their lending was justified by their vaunted risk analysis models.

The issue here is not about whether international lending should be stopped altogether. It is about quantity and concentration of debt. There is absolutely no justification for the fact that Bank of America, the second largest bank in the U.S., loaned $2.5 billion—*half of its capital*—to the country of Brazil. That essentially places the bank's fate in the hands of one unstable, inflation-ridden country. One explanation is that Bank of America figured it had the ability to predict what no one—not Mao, not Lenin, not the shah of Iran, not the Gironde during the French Revolution, in spite of their vastly superior information and political savvy—has ever been able to predict. "There is little, in fact, to suggest," wrote Euromarket expert Stephan Mendelsohn, "that computers represent any improvement on old Mr. Nathan Meyer Rothschild trundling about in his carriage, receiving his intelligence by carrier pigeon, and getting his sovereign risk analysis [the determination of whether a country is economically and politically able to repay debt] wonderfully right." The banks had somehow forgotten that credit had always been behavioral, not mechanistic.

The remarkable achievement on the banks' new weltanschauung was that it enabled them to ignore all the precepts of history, including the rather pointed lessons of the previous decade. But this was only the first, and grandest, absurdity upon which many smaller absurdities were built. The banks were not only trying to measure the unmeasurable, but they were doing it with information that was frequently sketchy, out of date, and sometimes completely wrong. Financial information on developing countries was often two years old; debt figures in Argentina and Brazil were actually falsified during the late 1970s and early 1980s; and there was no way at all to keep track of a developing country's short-term debt, a buildup of which is the surest sign that a country is in a financial crisis. There was in fact no reliable method to ascertain the single most important statistic of all—the "external debt profile" of a given Third World country—because there was simply no agency to provide such information. Foreign audits were notoriously unreliable, and companies often had multiple sets of financial statements, only the most favorable of which were shown to the banks. In short, the banks had all along been feeding their computers with substantial quantities of bad information.

Yet around the single, central paradox of the system the banks wove an extraordinarily sophisticated web of information and analysis. Since they had decided to disregard the forest in favor of the trees, the trees became the subject of intense, even obsessive scrutiny. The prime movers here were the big banks—Citibank invented "country risk analysis" in 1974—and their systems, opinions, and statistics had a pervasive impact on all international banks. Much of the information I processed for Cleveland Trust's loan committees came from those banks; their moral suasion in combination with the supposed sophistication of their information had a lot to do with Cleveland Trust and other regional banks participating in foreign loans.

Information is money. It always has been. Throughout history, fortunes have been made off the inevitable lag in communications. Rothschild found out about Waterloo by carrier pigeon. Baron Reuters similarly used carrier pigeons to bridge the telegraph delay between Germany and Belgium, reporting stock prices ahead of the wires. In England, the Hambros once cornered the black-crepe market in Copenhagen after receiving advance news from a sea captain that the queen of Denmark had died. The world of seaborne news, faulty telegraphs, pony express, and carrier pigeons has been replaced by what Walter Wriston has called "a completely integrated international financial and informational marketplace capable of moving money and ideas to any place on this earth in minutes." But the sheer speed of information has little or nothing to do with its quality; in fact the banks were making piles of short-term money using *bogus* information. The political and economic data flashing around the world's telecom networks with such blinding dispatch said that Brazil or the Philippines were marvelous risks. They said that you could make a large disbursement in a matter of minutes, and that you could make a great deal of interest income from it. The banks were inordinately impressed with this technology. But it really offered only the chance to get in deeper trouble faster than ever before.

As I worked through dozens of international credit checks and country studies, the realization gradually dawned upon me that I was operating at about five removes from the truth. Cleveland Trust had no foreign branches. Its officers traveled regularly, but mainly to make sales calls, and much of their "intelligence gathering" was done from the shelter of first-class hotels and expensive restaurants. It had no way to independently verify the information it was getting and upon which it was basing hundreds of millions of dollars in loans. Cleveland Trust was thus completely at the mercy of the larger system; it could verify neither country risk nor the reliability of a foreign audit. The ironic joke here is that for all of its lack of sophistication, Cleveland Trust's risk analysis fared no worse than that of the larger banks when the hammer came down in 1982 and 1983. That was because the premise was all wrong: none of the banks was exempt from history.

2

I BEGAN analyzing foreign credit in the middle of one of the wildest borrower's markets in history. I had been assigned to the Latin American Area of Cleveland Trust's International Division—a rather grandiose name for the three young bank officers who traveled the region. It was quickly apparent that Latin America was the place to be in 1978; nothing in the Third World could touch it for sheer loan volume. Brazil, Mexico, and Venezuela were among the top ten borrowing countries in the world. Mexico and Brazil alone were receiving over half of all loans made to the Third World in 1978. Venezuela's popularity was advancing in lockstep with its booming oil revenues, and Argentina was on the threshold of its longest and largest loan spree. Chile and Colombia were suddenly receiving more solicitations than they knew what to do with. Never before had the herd instinct of the international commercial banks been as pronounced as it was in Latin America in the late 1970s; not since the lending frenzy in Weimar Germany had anyone seen quite this degree of focused, collective optimism. And Cleveland Trust was profoundly caught up in it. Its outstanding loans in Latin America in 1978 were roughly $100 million—only four years later they would exceed $200 million. When I began work the bank was fresh from a "co-management" role in a $100-million syndicated loan to a major Brazilian chemical company. This was an enormously prestigious accomplishment in those days; the work of a bank that was trying hard to get itself recognized as a significant force in Latin America. Cleveland Trust had decided, on the basis of the same information that everyone else was getting, that Brazil, Mexico, and Venezuela were excellent, low-risk loan opportunities in one of the fastest growing areas of the world.

The carefully constructed misinformation network that permitted all this to happen was the product of the banks' experience of the 1970s and must be understood on those terms. I had arrived in the credit department not only in the middle of the big Latin lending boom, but also at what turned out to be the highwater mark of international banking to this day. I do not mean banking as it is traditionally measured. The dollar volume of lending in the next four years was to dwarf that of 1978. But for the banks and bankers themselves there was no year to rival 1978 for sheer eagerness, enthusiasm, and hope. Because no major defaults by foreign countries had occurred yet, 1978 was the last time a bright young banker could uncynically claim to believe that the system was working, or that it was a strategically and morally sound enterprise for moving the world's money from the haves to the have-nots. For a brief, shimmering historical moment, we had entered what George Orwell called "the paradise of little fat men"—a bland, comfortable world where nothing went really wrong.

This marvelous, reassuring illusion could not last. The international banks were to pass from the halcyon days of 1978 into the buzzsaw of 1979, when OPEC's second oil-price increase sent the Western world into a deep, inflationary recession that lasted three years before showing signs of recovery. It also pushed the Third World's oil bill from $26 billion in 1978 to the untenable level of *$67 billion* in 1980, making necessary the truly frightening volume of lending and refinancing that has characterized banking in the eighties. 1979 would be a harrowing year. After the brief calm that followed recovery from the first oil-price increase, the world was suddenly full of peril again. The events of that year read like a catalogue of disaster: inflation in the U.S. hit 13 percent, the highest rate since 1946; the dollar fell to abysmal lows as international currency traders, including American banks, speculated furiously against it; while the dollar weakened, a gold panic swept the world, and the price of gold rocketed past $800 an ounce before the close of the year; in November, President Carter admitted the shah of Iran into the United States, which prompted the seizure of American hostages in the U.S. embassy; in December, the Soviet Union invaded Afghanistan. And while all this was going on, U.S. interest rates, in the jitteriest and most fickle financial climate anyone could remember, shot through 20 percent.

1979 would present a brand-new, lethal world to the banks. The international debt market, in spite of the efforts of many banks to pretend otherwise, would never be quite the same. As Poland defaulted in 1981, and Brazil, Mexico, Argentina, Venezuela, and much of the non-OPEC developing world followed in 1982 and 1983, international lending began to look less like a risk-free bonanza and more like a trap. The fact that Cleveland Trust's—and the rest of the banks'—response to this new danger was to *increase* their lending—and not just to increase it but to increase it *geometrically*—is one of history's great pieces of illogic.

But in 1978 the financial markets were largely free from such worries. Viewed from boardrooms in Cleveland, Ohio, the world seemed to be a much simpler place. Indeed, the bank and its peers had convinced themselves that many of the problems created by the 1974 oil catastrophe had been mastered. The steep recession of 1974–1975 had been replaced by steady growth—4.5 percent in the U.S, 10 percent in Japan, 4 percent in the United Kingdom. The banking system had withstood the failures of two major international banks (Franklin National and Bankhaus I. D. Herstatt), a major panic in the Eurocurrency market, and the insolvencies of Indonesia, Peru, Turkey, and Zaire and had emerged stronger and more confident than ever. Bankers pointed to Chile as a model of the alleged resiliency of the system. It was one of the first international financial disasters of the 1970s, a country that creditors treated with embarrassed silence even in 1975. But by 1978 it was back in business and entertaining hundreds of eager creditors. Chileans had cut their annual inflation rate from 1,029 percent in 1974 to under 30 percent in 1978, thereby proving to the banks—which liked to view these things in general terms—that Latin America's problems were both short-term in nature and correctable by the application of basic monetarist principles. What Chile really proved was that bankers had short memories. As the decade wore on, their memories would seem to disappear entirely, as they studiously forgot all that they had learned.

The illusion of safety in 1978 was further aided by an extraordinary discovery the banks had made in dealing with Peru and Turkey. They found that the International Monetary Fund (IMF)—the hitherto maligned and apparently useless collection of multinational bureaucrats—could be used to shore up their fragile foreign loans. Indeed, it could be used to police the banks' credits, enforce their loan convenants, and—here was the real genius—underwrite foreign risk with taxpayers' money. Peru lit the way. It had had a brush with default in 1976 and 1977 after its foreign debt had risen from $1 billion in 1968 to $4.4 billion in 1975. Commercial banks had failed on their own to provide an adequate rescue package; the country was still unable to pay its debt, yet insisted upon the purchase of such things as $250-million worth of fighter-bombers from the Soviet Union, which its economy emphatically did not need. In desperation, the banks had then turned to the IMF, which, in exchange for the right to enforce a strict program of fiscal austerity, provided in August 1978 $200 million in new credit and handily restored creditor confidence in Peru. The Peruvian rescue finally came down to one stunning precedent that would forever affect the way the banks regarded foreign debt. The U.S. and Europe increased the IMF's lendable capital by $10 billion, an extraordinary sum that was funded by people who neither understood it at the time nor wanted it—the taxpayers.

The IMF's bail out of Peru in 1978 proved two hypotheses which the money center banks would later exploit with great success, and which Cleveland Trust, in its role as helpless second banana, would have to go along with. First, the IMF could be used, in effect, as a tool of international blackmail to force countries to implement policies favored by creditor banks, in exchange for the critical vote of confidence of the IMF. Second, the banks could scare Western governments into using public monies to shore up private lending. "Your strength is just an accident arising from the weakness of others," wrote Joseph Conrad in *Heart of Darkness*. He could have been talking about the IMF. Its use to rescue foreign debt was largely accidental in those early years; a wonderful, lucky break for the banks, who found themselves suddenly unable to bend sovereign wills to their own. In 1978, there was little reason for them to lean heavily—as they would later—on the IMF. That it existed as an additional safety net was simply another reason to keep on lending. But the precedent had been established, and the banks would never again, as economist Michael Moffitt wrote, "stray very far from the skirts of the IMF."

The "paradise of little fat men" existed in 1978 because the system had weathered all challenges; because where there should have been a panic, there had been none; because where there had been rough edges, the IMF had smoothed them over; because the financial apocalypse that the doom-prophets had been predicting refused to come. The banks that year were infused with notions of their own infallibility. They had been right after all, they told themselves, to lend those billions to the Third World after the 1973 oil shock.

"Paradise" was thus a state of mind. But there was also a practical reason for believing in the safety of world credit markets in 1977 and 1978: the banks were desperate to lend money. Because of the cheap money policies of the Western governments, commercial banks were now awash with funds. And because of the recession's limiting effect on corporate capital investment, they faced sluggish loan demand at home. The illusion of safety overseas allowed them to do what had previously been impossible: make relatively cheap international loans in large quantities. The multinational banks were fighting for the privilege of arranging large syndicated loans to Korea, Brazil, Algeria, and dozens of others, while hundreds of smaller banks like Cleveland Trust lined up to participate in those loans. The result was a frenzied, unorthodox "borrower's market" that had the banks hustling as they had never hustled before. "A few years ago no borrower would dream of the terms which can be obtained today on a rollover Eurocredit," wrote Kurt Richolt in March 1978. "Of $29.4 billion rollover Eurocredits syndicated in the 13 months from January 1977 until the end of January 1978, 37 percent commanded a spread of only 1 percent or slightly lower, and 13 percent had a margin of ¾ percent or less." These were astonishing terms, usually reserved for prime industrial countries. They had prompted sovereign borrowers—primarily Brazil, Mexico, the Philippines, South Korea, Morocco, and Portugal, which together accounted for three-quarters of all lending to non-OPEC Third World countries— to negotiate seven loans in excess of a billion dollars and twenty-nine loans exceeding three hundred million. The once-bitten-twice-shy attitude that had characterized international banking since the crisis of 1974 had given way to a quirky sort of ultraliberalism. The banks quickly and remorselessly began cutting their interest rates to secure a piece of the pie. Even South Korea, which a year before had paid 1¾ percent over the London Interbank Offered Rate (LIBOR) for seven-year money, could now borrow ten-year money at ¾ percent. Some bankers even claimed that they were losing money on their loans, which prompted the quip: "I lose a little bit on each transaction, but that's all right, because I make up for it in volume."

This last and most Dionysian phase of the international lending orgy thus began in 1978 with tremendous confidence, with the feeling, based on five years of hard times, that the system would weather all crises. The truth, which was hard to see then, was that the warning signals of an international debt crisis already abounded. Like Julius Caesar ignoring omens on the morning of his death, the banks chose to dismiss these signals as rank anomalies, unworthy of their consideration. In March 1978, international banking's principal organ, *Euromoney* magazine, ran a list of what it considered to be the world's problem loans. It was surprisingly long: Gabon, $2 billion; Peru, $4.4 billion; Portugal, $4.2 billion; Sudan, $1.5 billion; Turkey, $6.5 billion; Zaire, $1.2 billion;

Zambia, $562 million. "The fierce debates about debt levels," said the magazine in its January issue, "the scare headlines about the size of these debts, and the general dearth of credit information . . . had little or no effect on the willingness of the banks to keep on lending." Worse yet, 27 percent of the money being raised in 1978 by non-OPEC Third World countries was going to *refinance existing debt.* The loans of the early 1970s had matured and simply been subsumed in much larger borrowings. Already, the pattern was emerging: more and more new debt was going to pay off old, allowing the borrower, at the maturity of his loan, to pay no principal at all. Already in 1978, we were in the invidious world of the "rollover"—a term that describes the banks' practice of creating a new loan to pay off the old loan, rather than demanding payment in full. *Euromoney* and other journals were like Cassandra in the Greek myth: blessed with the gift of prophecy, but cursed by the fact that no one would believe it.

Since nothing had gone terribly wrong, this fool's paradise was an attractive place. Even slow-footed Cleveland Trust had been swept up on this great wave of confidence toward those low-risk profits across the sea. It was not the only conservative bank outside the money centers so affected. Big-time international lending was no longer, as it was in the early 1960s, the private domain of a small, exclusive club of huge multinational banks. The fad was to go global, and it had reached deep into provincial America. In 1960, only 8 U.S. banks had branches abroad, housing total assets of $3.5 billion. But the growth had been such that, by the beginning of 1978, 140 U.S. banks had 750 foreign branches, with $225 billion in assets. And these banks were coming to rely more and more on their overseas loans for profits. The domestic business of the top 13 U.S. banks had virtually stagnated through the first half of the decade, growing at a sluggish 4 percent. But foreign earnings had risen seven times, from 17 percent to 49 percent of total earnings.

You need only look at the banks' print advertisements that year to see the extent of this "going global" disease. Cleveland Trust said that it would do "just about anything to help [corporate clients] compete successfully in the world market place," and offered such services as export financing, Eurocurrency loans, foreign exchange contracts, and electronic funds transfer. The ads for Connecticut Bank and Trust, a much smaller regional bank than Cleveland Trust, claimed that the globe was "our region. Some regional banks," the ad continued, "confine their activities to just their own region. Which is fine as long as their customers do the same. At CBT, our customers do business around the world. And we go around the world to help.'' And then, smugly: ''It's not the easiest way for a regional bank to do business. But it's the best way.'' It would have been unheard of, even unthinkable, for a tiny regional bank to make such grandiose claims even five years before. And this was not just boilerplate: CBT desperately wanted, along with many other small banks, to enter the ranks of the big international lenders, and to proclaim this loudly on the doorsteps of their large U.S. corporate clients. The implication of such advertising was clear: In a viciously aggressive borrower's market, there was no holding back.

My own position in such a hyperactive debt market was peculiar, to say the least, and the fact the Cleveland Trust had put me there said a great deal about how the regional banks were approaching the business of foreign credit analysis in the late 1970s. I had had only a month of formal training in a credit class when the bank assigned me to the Latin American area of the international division, although I spoke no Spanish. The assumption, I suppose, was that I would somehow muddle through. But the idea of assigning a financial tyro to analyze million-dollar credits in a foreign language in which he has no fluency is bizarre indeed. It pointed up the general paucity of resources in the regional banks during the sustained lending boom of the middle and late 1970s. Expertise was thin, experience even thinner. The volume of lending had simply outstripped the ability of smaller banks to keep pace with it. It was a perpetual game of catch-up ball, played by all of the big regionals. The money center banks like Citibank, Chase, and Morgan Guaranty had been operating overseas since the first decades of the twentieth century. They set the pace of lending, and they pioneered the new lending markets. They also possessed large, stable, corporate infrastructures and sophisticated credit departments for handling foreign loans. As the money center banks became even more sophisticated, the ''information gap'' separating them from the regionals widened, and increasingly it became a game of follow the leader. Without any means of independent verification, the regionals could only assume that if all the big banks were doing it, then it must be all right.

Cleveland Trust was no exception. Its own resources were relatively minimal. The bank had been operating overseas only in the 1970s. Its pool of experts in Latin American affairs consisted of one thirty-two-year-old vice-president with a halting fluency in Spanish and Portuguese, two thirty-year-old assistant vice-presidents with a total of eight years banking experience between them, and me. I was technically under the supervision of an experienced analyst in the credit department—but he spoke no foreign languages at all, and, though he was well-schooled in certain areas of domestic credit, he had no idea what to do with, say, the effects of a massive currency devaluation on a Brazilian company's balance sheet. This could be a very tricky problem, particularly for someone who had just learned for the first time what a fixed asset was, and who could never be quite sure if he was translating the language of those statements correctly in the first place. I was more or less on my own in a fast market that did not permit the luxury of slow and leisurely apprenticeship.

Cleveland Trust's babe-in-the-woods approach to foreign credit was partly the result of its natural aversion to things international, partly the result of the disparity between the full-tilt loan solicitations of the ninth floor and the more steady, prosaic growth of the credit department. But the bank had none of these problems in its domestic lending areas. Although it lacked the resources of the New York, Chicago, and California banks, it gave nothing away to them when it came to good-old-fashioned nuts-and-bolts American lending, which it had been doing with consistent success since 1895. And it was not uncommon in the domestic corporate bank for a young analyst to be turned loose with multimillion-dollar credits; the sink-or-swim practice was in fact a bank tradition. On the domestic side of the bank, this was a perfectly good idea. So deep was the bank's domestic expertise that a significant mistake by a rookie analyst would be quickly perceived by most of the bank's middle managers. If the analyst happened to be working with insurance companies or tool-and-die makers, he was certain to encounter several senior vice-presidents who had spent thirty years making loans like that. The benefits of the sink-or-swim policy were obvious. If the credit analyst had talent, you made him a loan officer. If he did not, you exiled him to "credit correspondence" or some other unpleasant place until he could not stand it anymore and quit.

But things were different in International, where the bank had confused its domestic credit policies with its foreign ones. The same principles applied, but now in a vacuum. There was no significant school of thought at the bank against which my analyses of Latin American countries or companies could be measured, no old hand who had spent his life lending to Latin America who could act as final arbiter. Most of the credit work in the past had been seat-of-the-pants stuff, and it had been done by the handful of people who were now running those loans on the ninth floor. And they had most certainly been flying blind back in the early 1970s. When I joined the credit department there were two other analysts assigned to the international division. Between them, they had one undergraduate economics degree, one Russian degree, and three months of banking experience. The bank was relying simply on its wits and common sense. For example, one of the types of Latin American companies I had to analyze was called a *financiera,* a Latin hybrid of savings and loan society, commercial bank, and finance company. No member of Cleveland Trust's senior loan committee—the guys who could take apart a three-year revolving-credit-convertible-to-term loan for a local construction company in five minutes and find every weak point— had ever in his wide experience encountered a *financiera.* The loan committee did not therefore have any framework within which to examine the credit risk. There was no way for them to interpret the financial figures. My supervisor did not speak Spanish or Portuguese, nor did he understand foreign accounting practices; and the account officers on the ninth floor were too busy selling loans to spend much time with it. All this meant that they had to trust me—to some extent, anyway— and that I had to trust the information network that produced the data I analyzed.

3

LET US consider how the information system of international credit actually operated at Cleveland Trust in 1978. Credit, because it deals in the rather slippery concept of "confidence," is thoroughly human, and therefore unreliable. So it is appropriate to begin with the human beings who made the decisions that moved the bank's money to foreign shores.

The point man in Cleveland Trust's Latin operation—and my immediate boss—was Rick Herrick, a driven thirty-two-year-old vice-president who in spite of his age was one of the old-timers of the bank's international division. He occupied the desk next to Charles Hammel's along the back wall of the ninth floor, and for the seven or eight months a year that he was not on the road he could be found at that desk six days a week, staring stoically down at his paperwork, surrounded by an absurdly high stack of credit files, international journals, memos, and "tickets" from loan committee meetings. Herrick was an interesting case. Like Hammel, he was primarily a traveling salesman. Yet there was nothing of the hale-fellow-well-met in Rick Herrick, none of the back-slapping flamboyance or casual intimacy of the born salesman. He had compensated for this by the sheer driving relentlessness with which he pursued his quarry throughout the Third World. It would have been difficult to find a loan officer anywhere who had made as many foreign calls as Herrick had in the preceding six years. He had pounded on more doors, in more countries, and under more adverse conditions than anyone else. He came from a good family, of course—this was almost de rigueur on the ninth floor—had been to several prestigious boarding schools, and wore the standard, loosely tailored, slightly dowdy Brooks Brothers clothing that was the hallmark of his class.

In the preceding year, Herrick had pulled off what most of the people on the ninth floor considered a major political coup. He had gotten himself transferred from the relatively static lending zones of the Asia Pacific area to the hyperkinetic markets of Latin America, and in so doing he had landed in a veritable lender's paradise. He had been given two underlings to help him pursue his foreign business—a tiny feat of empire expansion that none of the other foreign area managers had achieved—which was a singularly clear signal, amid the confusing, ambiguous, and often inchoate ones that came down from above, that the bank was hungry for new business. Dozens of large Cleveland Trust clients were operating in South America, and the banking world had already given the area its blessing as the prime borrowing risk of the 1970s.

So Herrick would drive the credit machine. He would scout and solicit the business that would be brought before the bank's loan committees. The committees had the power to reject his business, of course, but the loan selection would always be Herrick's. And thus did Herrick, quite unwittingly, become the first clearing point in the vast network of misinformation that was operating full-bore in Latin America in 1978.

Within the confines of the ninth floor, Herrick was simply a banker. Out in the civilized wilds of Brazil, Argentina, or Chile, he became a salesman in the purest sense of the word. He had a grueling agenda of six or seven customer calls a day, often in remote parts of a foreign city, often including a business lunch and business dinner each day. Herrick did not linger on the beaches of Rio de Janeiro or in the bistros of Caracas after a week of manic solicitations. More likely, he would be on one of the dangerous red-eye specials over the Andes, flying through

time zones, writing call reports, and reading political and economic intelligence when he was not actually calling on customers.

Part of Herrick's job—an extremely important part as far as the bank
was concerned—was to retrieve information about the countries in which
the bank did business. But this function collided head-on with what
Herrick was actually doing out there, which was selling the bank's loans
and services. His job would never be measured by how correct his country risk analysis was. At the very least, Herrick was simply doing what
hundreds of other larger international banks had already done, and any
ultimate blame for poor forecasting would be shared by tens of thousands of bankers around the world; this was one of the curious benefits of following the herd. Herrick's performance would, however,
be measured by how many loans he made, and thus his trips were
heavy on solicitation and short on "information gathering." This was
not Herrick's fault. His budget, among other things, did not allow for
it.

The information he brought back consisted of what he had seen of
the country and of what he had heard in his conversations with local
officials and businessmen. The former was necessarily limited because
of his crowded, hectic agenda. Most of his experience of a given country consisted of getting to and from airports, grabbing taxicabs at rush
hour, sitting in customers' offices or touring their plants, and eating
meals in hotels. In that sense, his feel for the country would be slightly
narrower than that of the average tourist, who at least has the option of
random wandering and discovery. And while his local conversations
produced a considerable amount of local business intelligence—leads
for new business and that sort of thing—they produced very little hard
information about the actual state of the country. The most popular in-
telligence-gathering grounds for Herrick and most international bankers
in those years were the central banks, which made sense for they were
the ultimate sources of all economic and financial information on a
country. But in fact the loan salesmen could not have chosen a more
biased, self-serving, or bureaucratic environment to hunt for their hard
facts. The actual meeting with the central-bank functionary was often
nothing more than an exercise in international politesse. The functionary
did not deal in bad news; that was counterproductive. He purveyed only
the sunniest of current statistics. If the question you wanted answered
was, Should I make a seven-year, $30-million unsecured loan in this
country? then you were asking the wrong man. In the Third World,

considerations of nationalism inevitably took precedence over those of accuracy.

The commercial banks had zeroed in on foreign central banks largely in the absence of any other reliable reporting institution. As a colleague of mine observed later, "Who the hell else were you going to ask?" The only other possibility that came to mind was the U.S. embassy's economic attaché, who was only slightly less bureaucratic and sheltered than the central-bank officials, and whose access to financial statistics was severely limited. The question remained: If you wanted accurate, up-to-date, inside knowledge of a country, who would provide it? The six o'clock news? Politicians? Religious leaders? Academics? Bankers? Businessmen? The answer—assuming you could get one at all—might involve a combination of all of those things, and that was patently impossible for someone with a business agenda as jammed as Herrick's. So it was more or less by default that the central banks had been chosen, and as years went by they came to accept this function with greater and greater relish. It was, among other things, a means of control. As the second oil price increase took effect, especially in the non-oil-producing countries, it was increasingly in their interest to manipulate the information their creditors got.

Herrick's "call reports" from these information-gathering meetings were usually brief and extraordinarily dull. He was obviously walking through what he as an intelligent man considered a necessary but inane task. He asked questions to which he already knew the answers, or to which there were no real answers at all. In an hour-long meeting over tea and biscuits with an affluent bureaucrat who represented his country's highest social class, there was nothing else he could do. Topics such as social revolution were simply not discussed in such genteel circles—unless, of course, such an event was already in progress.

Cleveland Trust's upper management did not see it this way. They did not believe that the *Wall Street Journal* was a better intelligence source than five hundred conversations over tea with central bank officials, although this was often true. Nor did they see that what they were really doing was playing the old game of follow the leader. Their true justification for making loans in Brazil, Venezuela, or Mexico had nothing to do with their own or Herrick's efforts to gather country information. Cleveland Trust had made its move into Latin America long after the waters had been tested by dozens of large American and foreign banks. The bank was simply moving with the herd. That Herrick and his colleagues checked in from time to time with foreigners—whose primary commitments were to their countries' well-being, with the truth coming second—was merely a sop to the consciences of the men in the executive suites on the twenty-sixth floor. It cannot be said that Herrick retrieved bad information, which was delivered in other, more sophisticated forms, but that he brought back no information on the country's political or social stability that could not be gotten from a reasonably well-staffed news service.

But of course Herrick was mainly a calling officer, not a political scientist or economist. He called on a variety of prospects. There were the local banks, with whom Cleveland Trust did short-term and documentary business, and with whom it was important to maintain good relations. Then there were the U.S. multinationals, which were Cleveland Trust's main source of business: companies such as Goodyear, Firestone, Eaton, Dana, Harris, General Electric, and Diamond Shamrock. On Herrick's hunting map of Latin America these names would always figure prominently, it was this sort of business that his bosses said they wanted most of all. Also on the list were foreign government agencies, or nationalized corporations like Pemex in Mexico, or Petrobras or Electrobras in Brazil, who were purchasers of U.S. goods and services. Finally, there were the ordinary indigenous foreign corporations that bought American products. Herrick's job was really to follow U.S. trade—to map its routes and sales patterns and follow them to the doorstep of the buyer, who usually needed financing. Almost everyone in the Third World needed financing in the 1970s, and most of the big money had to come from abroad. A successful three-week trip might produce a dozen "leads"—financing opportunities that had yet to be ratified by Cleveland Trust's credit establishment. Herrick's lending authority was a mere $1 million for terms of less than one year—an extremely modest sum for 1978, and one which meant little or nothing to anything resembling a major borrower.

So Herrick would return with his impressions of the countries he had visited, his taped call reports, and a suitcase stuffed with paper that documented his leads. Within a week of his arrival, much of this material would land on my desk for "spreading and analysis." Most of it would be marked "RUSH." And thus began the laborious and urgent task of preparing this abstract information for presentation to the loan committees.

My job was to write a comprehensive risk analysis, both of the prospective borrower and of its country. My work would be reviewed and modified by Herrick, then presented by him to two separate loan committees for approval. But before I even began my analysis—and quite independent of any conclusions I might come to about either the country or the borrower—I confronted the single largest contradiction of the international lending business, one whose ultimate effect would be to cause over a hundred million dollars in Cleveland Trust loans to Latin America to go sour. This had to do with what was known in banker's jargon as "convertibility risk."

In foreign lending there are two distinct types of risk: that of the borrower itself as an ongoing enterprise, and that of the country in which the borrower is located. If the loan is made directly to a sovereign government, then the two are one and the same. But if the borrower is a private foreign company, or a subsidiary of a U.S. multinational, then the risks must be considered separately. A company can go bankrupt, or fail to repay a loan, in the healthiest of political and economic environments. This is obvious. What is not so obvious, however, and what was inexplicably overlooked by Cleveland Trust and many other U.S. banks, was that a foreign borrower was only as solvent as its country of domicile. A Brazilian company that borrows dollars from a U.S. bank to help it earn cruzeiros in the local market must eventually take those cruzeiros to the Brazilian Central Bank and exchange them for dollars in order to repay its loan. If the country of Brazil is out of dollars, the company will default on its loan, no matter how many cruzeiros it has, or how profitable and healthy it is. This is "convertibility risk": the possibility that a foreign company may not be able to convert local currency to dollars to repay foreign debt. Inconvertibility was to be the fate of most of the private-sector debt held by U.S. banks in Latin America in 1982 and 1983.

In Latin America the convertibility risk had been historically high. Since the late nineteenth century the area had followed a boom-to-bust pattern, driven by the excessive reliance on a few commodities: coffee in Brazil, copper and other minerals in Peru, fruit in Central America, and fishing in Peru. This had been exacerbated since mid-century, especially in Venezuela, Brazil, and Mexico, by the growing phenomenon of "flight capital"—the expatriation of local currency by foreign nationals into U.S. dollar accounts in the U.S. and Europe.

A brief glance at the history books, then, would have warned the banks of the Latin countries' chronic aptitude for running out of foreign currency. But for all their computerized risk models, and for all of their protestations of awareness of the convertibility factor, they behaved as though a new age had dawned on the continent. Their first error, as I have pointed out, was to believe that they could predict with reasonable accuracy a country's political and economic conditions seven or ten years into the future. That they did believe this was evidenced by the extraordinary quantity of long-term loans they were making in Latin America and in the rest of the Third World in the 1970s, often at extremely low rates of interest. This included both private and public-sector debt. If you open a copy of *Euromoney* or the *Institutional Investor* from 1978, you will be amazed at the quantity of "tombstones" (advertisements by banks proclaiming their participation in major international loans) published by big commercial banks gloating over such things as a seven-year, $1-billion multicurrency "facility" to the Federal Republic of Nigeria; or a $1.2-billion seven-year credit to the United Mexican States; or a $310-million medium-term loan to the National Petrochemical Company of Iran. These announcements were considered to be the apogee of prestige in the international banking business in the late 1970s and early 1980s.

But given this mystifying, illogical premise, the banks then went ahead and compounded the error with a far more serious breach of their traditional credit policies: They placed no upper limit on the amount any country or company could borrow from the banking system. By neglecting to do so, they took what was already a dangerous game of convertibility risk and transformed it into a sort of Russian roulette. One of the first things that any banker learns in a credit class is how to legally restrict his borrower from taking on excessive debt. The idea is simple and sound: the more the borrower becomes indebted to other lenders, the more the original loan is in jeopardy. Banks perfect these restrictions in the form of "loan covenants" which specifically state how much additional debt the borrower can take on. If the borrower exceeds this, then he is in "default"—and the bank can "accelerate maturity," causing the full amount of the loan to be due and payable immediately. Such covenants are among the oldest and most standard practices of the banking industry.

The international banks faithfully tied up private-sector borrowers in Latin America with these covenants; but they utterly neglected it at the sovereign level. That was why Brazil and Mexico could run up $80 or $90 billion in total debt, or a struggling country like Argentina could borrow more than $40 billion. Technically, the debt could have hit hundreds of billions in each country before the final reckoning; there was no way, legal or otherwise, to stop it. The banks' legal lending limits ranged between 10 and 15 percent of their capital and reserves to a single borrower, and while this limited an individual bank's exposure to an individual borrower, it said nothing about how much a country could borrow *in aggregate*. The banks were also forbidden to concentrate more than 15 percent of their total loan portfolios in a single country—but again, this set no explicit upper limit on a country's total borrowings. The commercial banks could have—and still have—insisted on "ceilings" for borrowers, but they were too busy competing for a piece of the action. The U.S. regulatory authorities could have made a rule of it, but for some reason did not. In any case the U.S. Comptroller of the Currency would have had no power over a foreign bank.

Countries were thus treated as though they were not single, discrete borrowing entities, and this was radically wrong. All of the debt was being taken on in dollars and was repayable in dollars. Cleveland Trust had no use for billions of cruzeiros. That some of the borrowers were in the private sector and some in the public ceased to have any meaning when it came to ultimate repayment: all borrowers had to change local currency for dollars at their countries' central banks. By disregarding this, the banks virtually insured that their optimistic predictions would not come true. And as they climbed over one another to pump more and more debt into the country, they were increasingly endangering the loans they had already made.

Herrick's lead on a loan to a multinational subsidiary in Chile, for example, was in a sense doomed from the start—before I even began to translate the figures. Because Herrick had no control over the total borrowings of Chile, it was impossible to say with any certainty what the convertibility risk would be in one, two, or seven years. The effect was exactly as though he were omitting debt covenants from his loan agreements.

On these nonsensical premises, then, I undertook my analysis of foreign risk. From my position, it would have been useless to question the existence of the emperor's new clothes. I was the tiniest of cogs in an enormous system that seemed to be working marvelously well, and in which most of my superiors at the bank had invested a great deal of personal capital. And once I had accepted the largest absurdities of the system, it was much easier to handle the smaller ones, which would only double and redouble and grow more ingenious as I progressed through my analyses.

My logical starting point in a foreign loan was the country study itself, since the bank understood, on a primitive level anyway, that a loan to a country that was about to explode in Marxist rebellion was a bad idea. I had never been anywhere in Latin America except to Mexico City for a week's vacation a few years before. But my own experience was unimportant anyway because the international banking system in 1978 was loaded with published "intelligence" from banks, government agencies, and private services about every country on earth. All I had to do was read as much of it as I could find, cull the important facts, and arrange them in a neat three-page format for the leisurely digestion of the loan committees.

Much of this information—which carried the full authority of the world's major financial institutions—was either outdated, incomplete, or simply wrong. This was not widely known in 1978. It was not until the debt crisis began that the unreliability of these figures became known. This was not because the information was too bulky or too opaque, but because the banks had never cared to look at it too closely.

Country intelligence consisted mainly of numbers. These numbers dealt with all aspects of a foreign country, but above all they were meant to show a country's balance of payments and its ability to pay back foreign debt. The concept is astonishingly simple, and much easier to grasp than the big banks' risk experts would have you believe. First, the world runs on U.S. dollars. That is how virtually all Third World debts, trade payments, and transfers are denominated. A Venezuelan bolivar, a Brazilian cruzeiro, or a Mexican peso are worth absolutely nothing outside of their home countries. No one will accept them in payment for anything. The dollar is not the world's only hard currency—Swiss francs, British pounds sterling, German marks, and Japanese yen are also "hard"—but for all practical purposes the dollar is the currency of international trade. From a lender's point of view, a country's creditworthiness has to do with only one thing: that country's ability to earn or attract U.S. dollars. And so the first and most important item to be measured in country risk analysis is what is known as the "current account": imports, exports, and transfer payments, which consist largely of workers' remittances and government grants. If a country imports more than it exports, there is a net drain on its dollar accounts; conversely, it accumulates dollars by exporting more than it imports. Any country that, over the long term, is a net importer of goods will eventually run out of both dollars and the ability to borrow them, and it is therefore a bad credit risk. Period.

The second item in the balance of payments account is known as "capital transfers." This covers all loans made into the country, and all loans or investments that are made overseas by residents of the country. When you add the net current account to the net capital transfers, you get the country's net inflow or outflow of dollars. Analysis of this figure over a period of years is the single most important consideration in foreign lending—and even the most naïve outsider could have told you on the basis of these figures that in the early 1980s Third World debt was in trouble. Brazil, for example, had run a large current account deficit in the mid-1970s caused by the country's huge import bill for oil and manufactured goods. In those years, this deficit was compensated by foreign loans. But between 1979 and 1982, Brazil's $24 billion in foreign borrowings was more than offset in the capital transfers account by interest payments to foreign banks of $28 billion. The country was still running a large current account deficit, but was now actually bleeding cash even though its international debt was rising.

The last important statistical category was the country's "external debt profile." This means, quite simply, how much the country owes in long- and short-term debt to foreign banks and governments, and how much yearly interest and principal it is required to pay. The analytic device that makes sense of this is known as the "debt service ratio"— which relates total debt payments in a single year to a country's receipts from goods and services, much like the ratio your bank runs on your income to see if you are worthy of a mortgage—and was the most widely used ratio in international banking.

My first stop in the bogus information network was thus to turn to the official published sources of these statistics. In view of the importance the bank placed on them—and the fact that almost all international credit ratings were derived from them—I was amazed to find that in using them, it was impossible to come up with an accurate picture of a country's external debt profile, its debt service ratio, or its capital transactions account. (Still, I had no idea then of how inaccurate the numbers really were.)

Let us begin with the external debt profile. It would seem simple enough to find out how much a country has borrowed—it would seem necessary, in fact, that the banks know exactly what that figure was.

But there was no central clearinghouse for this information. The great achievement of the Euromarkets had been to place much of international lending outside sovereign control, its great failing was that there had never been any reliable way to keep track of Eurodollar lending in the less-developed world. Thus the banks could never be sure, at any given moment, how much debt a country had. The industrialized countries were much more sophisticated in reporting their own financial statistics. But information on the Third World, particularly in the late 1970s, was far less accurate. The only approximation of a "natural reporting entity" for the banks was a sort of supercentral bank in Switzerland called the Bank for International Settlements (BIS). All estimates on the size of the Euromarket—including specific loan amounts in specific countries—come from the BIS, which gets the information from the banks themselves. But the statistics come out at what is estimated, conservatively, to be a four- to seven-month time lag. And, in the words of the *Institutional Investor*'s Darrell Delamaide,

> none of these statistics are refined enough or fast enough to catch a buildup of short-term credits, which is exactly what precipitated the Mexican payments crisis. No single agency or bank has firsthand information on all types of credit—bilateral, military, export, Euromarket, medium-term, short-term. Oddest of all, perhaps, is that until the crisis itself, only a few central banks had any idea of the overall involvement of their commercial banks in international loans.

The banks' inability to track a country's short-term credits was probably the most alarming weakness in the system. Short-term credit refers mainly to borrowings by central banks, commercial banks, and corporations under 180 days. Often, these short-term debts are continuously rolled over, meaning that they are actually thinly disguised term loans. When a country such as Brazil, Mexico, or Venezuela runs into serious financial trouble, it finds that its long-term credit sources—the banks and investors who were once willing to put up five-, seven-, or ten-year money—will rapidly dry up. In desperation, the country's financial institutions begin to draw heavily—and usually not in concert—upon their short-term lines of credit. This is the last, and unavoidable, act of a desperate sovereign borrower that, shut off from its usual capital markets, has no other choice. Bankers professed both shock and amazement at the enormity of the short-term debt of both Brazil and Mexico after the countries had failed to make payment on foreign debt. It was finally obvious that they had no way of keeping track of it—no means of ascertaining the most telling signal of imminent sovereign bankruptcy. So ignorant were they that less than two months before Mexico ran out of hard currency altogether in August 1982, Bank of America had signed up thirty-five banks to participate in a $2.5-billion loan to a government finance corporation, the Nacional Financiera. The BIS was unable to monitor the figures, and the central banks of the reporting countries simply would not publish them, either through inefficency or an outright intent to deceive.

The next most likely place to look for foreign debt figures was the International Bank for Reconstruction and Development, popularly known as the World Bank. The World Bank kept a voluminous record of world borrowings in the form of "World Debt Tables," and a separate tally of the debt service ratios. These were widely considered by the banks, including Cleveland Trust, as accurate figures, and were incorporated into country studies as such. The problem here was that while the tables faithfully recorded public-sector and government-guaranteed debt, albeit at a far greater lag than even the BIS, they omitted altogether the private debt obligations that did not carry a public guarantee. While this figure has little or no application in socialist, centrally planned economies such as Poland or Algeria, it is extremely significant in countries such as Brazil, Mexico, Argentina, and Venezuela, all of which have active, well-developed private sectors which borrowed on the international market. Half of Cleveland Trust's loans to Brazil and Mexico were to the private sector. The World Bank figures ignored the fact that when it came to converting currency, the economic pluralism of a country suddenly disappeared, as all borrowers—public and private—had to exchange local currency for dollars at the same central bank. This was not an oversight by the World Bank: the numbers were simply not available.

The third significant source of country information was the International Monetary Fund, which supplied very little in the way of hard debt information but did record a great deal of dated and incorrect information provided by the countries themselves. "In the case of less developed countries," wrote Stephan Mendelsohn in 1980, "statistics are dated, partial, and provide guidance only of the crudest kind. Information about external debt is usually 2 years out of date, and usually excludes military debt, which is often large. Quite fundamental data are sometimes madly wrong: the first census of the United Arab Emirates in 1975 disclosed a population 60 percent larger than supposed."

Another peculiar bit of news that came from the IMF (and the Organization for Economic Cooperation and Development in Paris) in those years was that the world's "balance sheet"—the statistical aggregates of all reporting countries, excluding those in the Warsaw Pact—was horrendously out of balance. In theory, one country's export, whether it be of goods, services, or capital, must be another country's import. These figures on a world scale should then net out to zero: liabilities plus capital equal assets. But they do not. They don't even come close. As late as 1982, the world was running an inexplicable deficit of $100 billion with itself. There have always been some discrepancies, to be sure; typically, they would be accounted for by illegal imports such as cocaine, or by illegal capital movements such as occurred out of France when the Socialists came to power. But as Vivian Brownstein wrote in *Fortune* magazine in 1983, the size of this deficit—this accounting error, if you will—"casts doubt on the current account balance reported by every country." Thus even the most basic statistics that I put in my country studies were wrong. They had to be: the world could not be that out of balance with itself. And the basic import-export figures were perhaps the most important single item in foreign credit analysis.

To complicate all this was the inability or unwillingness of certain countries in the Third World to keep track of their own debt. The *Nation* magazine reported in November 1982 that "Brazil's currency reserves were down to zero—perhaps even below zero—" yet "the country had kept itself going by the use of 'creative accounting' to inflate its foreign currency holdings." This is a kind way of saying that Brazil had lied about its reserve position. And in the meantime, the banks were making loans based on figures that were off by billions or even tens of billions of dollars.

But the most mysterious and least traceable of all Third World economic phenomena is known as "capital flight," which many believe was the single most destructive force of all in the late 1970s and early 1980s. It describes the process whereby a foreign national converts his local currency into dollars or some other hard currency and exports it in the form of investments, bank deposits, real estate, or consumer items purchased abroad. Wealthy Latin Americans have been doing this for decades, and one can hardly blame them. With the chronic inflation of most of Latin America, and the relative worthlessness of many of its currencies, it was far better to hold any long-term investments in the form of dollars. You and I would do the same, particularly if the economic climate was worsening, and if we were able to change our local currency at an artificial, government-subsidized rate. The BIS estimates that at least $50 billion slipped out of the region in this way from 1978 to 1982. So when the local officials began to wonder where the dollars were, one of the answers was that they had entered the country in the form of large syndicated loans, had been sold to wealthy locals at rates subsidized by those same loans, and then put in interest-earning deposits at U.S. and European banks—the same banks that had lent them in the first place. The U.S. bank thus ended up with both an unproductive government loan and a liability on its own books to a foreign national. Like a country's short-term debt position, capital flight was nearly impossible for anyone outside the foreign central bank to track.

The statistics in my country study, then, on which Cleveland Trust would justify millions of dollars of loans, did not include either current short-term or private-sector debt. They did not include any current figures on the rate or amount of capital flight. And the estimates of external debt position were often wrong by billions of dollars. There was no caveat to this effect in my country study; no one on the loan committees knew the figures were missing.

After I had consulted the statistics published by the international agencies, I would then turn to private publications to see how the financial world was interpreting these false or dated numbers. For "moral authority" I was usually pointed toward the publications issued by the big U.S. commercial banks, who had an increasingly keen interest in keeping the level of optimism high. There were many of these, and some, like Chase, actually sold country intelligence reports, which went into greater detail than their weekly or monthly pamphlets. All of the big banks, since they had been criticized by the IMF in the mid-1970s for their lack of systematic risk analysis programs, had developed sophisticated, computerized risk models, which were patrolled by large, salaried staffs. In the regionals this was far less true; Cleveland Trust is a prime example. In the absence of their own systems, the regionals paid close attention to what the big banks said. They had no other recourse, except to spend a lot of money to achieve what would presumably be the same end.

Because of the authority the big banks imparted to the smaller ones—who, after all, would come up collectively with most of the foreign loan money—they are perhaps the worst culprits of all in the bogus information network. They were habitually and uncannily wrong about most of the countries they analyzed, and not just in the long term. As they stumbled blindly toward the debt crisis, their records became even more disgraceful.

Their analysis of Mexico in the twelve months preceding the crisis provides a clear example of how dangerously misleading the big banks' information was, especially to regionals like Cleveland Trust which had no foreign branches to serve as listening posts. In Manufacturers Hanover Trust's December 1981 newsletter, "Byline"—two months before a radical currency devaluation and eight months before the country became completely insolvent—one of its Mexico-based officers was quoted as saying that the country was "probably one of the most dynamic economies in the world today. . . . The tremendous oil revenues—more than 70 percent of total income—also enable Mexico to insulate itself from many of the problems plaguing other developing nations. Government and industry alike encourage foreign investment and offer attractive incentives."

In 1981, Chase Manhattan's "International Financial Newsletter" neglected to mention growing evidence of an oil glut, capital flight, and other economic storm warnings, and asserted that "Growth in the current year is expected to remain in the 7.5 percent range as the oil output rate continues to rise and as agricultural output improves in response to added investment." Bank of America used double-paged advertisements to proclaim its lead role in a $2.5-billion acceptance financing facility for Pemex, the national oil company. "Today," the ad said, "Mexican industry is developing dynamically in many different directions. Our knowledge of the local business terrain can be invaluable. So if you're interested in Mexican business opportunities of any kind—talk to Bank of America." Still more invidious, a Bank of America officer was quoted in August of 1982 as saying, "We're telling our clients that now is a great time to lay foundations [in Mexico] for 1983 and beyond." That was only a few weeks before Mexico ran out of money. How could Bank of America have believed that? Surely with a local branch they must have known about the capital flight. Surely anyone could see what the radical drop in the price of oil was doing to Mexico's foreign exchange earnings. Surely Bank of America must have known the extent of Mexico's debt service requirements in 1982. Were the bank's officers naïve? Had they decided that, in view of their huge exposure in Mexico, it was in their interest to keep as many banks as possible in the game? For if regional and foreign banks began to pull lines of credit and refused to roll over short-term debt Bank of America's own position would be jeopardized. Whatever the reason, the advice was bad. If you had followed it in August 1982 you almost certainly would have lost money.

Big American banks were not the only purveyors of bad advice. One of the largest British banks, Lloyds Bank International, published a highly regarded monthly pamphlet called the *Bank of London and South America Review*. Its analyses of Brazil and Mexico in 1982 are written in a bland, phlegmatic bankspeak, and to read them in the months preceding the crises you would never know that anything was wrong in Latin America. Listen to this concluding segment of analysis in the Brazilian section published in November 1982, just a few weeks before Brazil ran out of money:

> Effective economic and financial management has been practiced in Brazil since the March 1964 revolution, and in particular close co-ordination and control of monetary, fiscal, and exchange policy instruments exists to a greater extent than in any other Latin American country. Some success has been experienced up to now in external debt management, which is based on improving the maturity profile and encouraging Resolution 63 operations. The underlying resilience of the country's economy and its longstanding and proven development record suggest that prospects for overcoming current difficulties brought on largely by exogenous factors must be relatively favourable.

This was the considered opinion of one of the world's largest and most powerful banks, which had a long history of foreign banking. If the point of the *Bank of London and South America Review* was truly to inform its readers of the economic situation in Brazil, then it should have been screaming bloody murder in November 1982. If its purpose was to maintain an artificial climate of optimism, then its analysis succeeded splendidly. (Oddly, though, by this time even the small regional banks knew that trouble was on its way in Brazil.)

Thus was the ''moral authority'' to make large, low-interest foreign loans conveyed upon the smaller banks by the bigger banks, who should have known better, and perhaps did know better, at least at some deeper level of perception.

As I wrote my country study, all of this information—IMF international financial statistics, World Bank debt tables, BIS reports, bank newsletters, and private intelligence reviews—would be arrayed before me, just as it was arrayed in some form before foreign credit analysts around the world. It was a very large pile of information, and most of the statistics confirmed each other, for they had all come from the same erroneous sources. My report was what it claimed to be: an accurate distillation of what the world's commercial banks thought about a given country at a certain point in time. There was nowhere else to look for the truth, and no one cared anyway.

I would then deliver my country study to Herrick, who would examine it for errors, omissions, or excessive bad news. Because Herrick's job was to make loans, he would purge from my studies any unnecessarily pessimistic speculation about the country's future, while diligently keeping in the sort of bland, optimistic generalizations that one found in the *Bank of London and South America Review*. Herrick's point, which I would later appreciate when I became a loan officer, was that you could always find alarmist things to say about a Third World country. He was right. One of the items that was removed from my studies was the projection that in the year 2000, thirty million people would be living in Mexico City. In my interpretation, no matter how much oil revenue Mexico pulled in, the government would not be capable of spreading the benefits among that many people, and that this in turn would increase the chances for social revolution. But in the business of making loans, Herrick said, you simply could not dwell on that sort of information. Otherwise nothing would get done. This was an important practical side to the lending business. Herrick's job was to put as many loans on the books as he could. If the bank did not want to lend in Mexico, then he would stop traveling there. As long as it did, he was merely impeding progress by saying terrible things about Mexico while the rest of the world's banks lined up to make loans to it. In practical terms, his logic was flawless; the idle doom prophecies of a junior analyst could only harm the system. Herrick had not been hired as a visionary. He had been hired to sell loans. And I had been hired to help him.

With an optimistic, well-researched country study in hand, Herrick and I would then proceed to the next phase—the analysis of the foreign borrower itself. Cleveland Trust made loans chiefly to four types of foreign companies: banks, both government and privately owned; government corporations such as Petrobras in Brazil or Pemex in Mexico; multinationals such as Goodyear Argentina or Firestone de Chile; and multinational joint ventures such as Vidriolux, S.A. in Venezuela, a partnership between General Electric and Venezuelan investors.

Here we encountered an entirely new set of problems with the quality of "microeconomic" information. With government corporations, you had to worry about how the money was being used. There was, for example, the pernicious phenomenon of "pass-through," whereby a foreign government uses its borrowing agencies as general rather than specific conduits for loan money. You may have loaned money for a hydroelectric plant, only to find that some or all of the money had found its way into one of the central bank's currency subsidy pools. Pemex, Mexico's national oil company, was a good example of this. Although it was resolutely treated by the foreign banks as an independent agency of the Mexican government, it was in fact nothing more than a conduit; at the end of each financial year, Pemex's profit statement read zero, the money having been "upstreamed" into government networks. Billions of dollars in loans were made to Pemex for drilling, exporting, etc., but the banks were never in a position to track their money all the way from disbursement to its actual employment to purchase, say, a drilling rig. There were many other examples of this phenomenon around the world. In Eastern Europe, for example, foreign banks had no way at all to control the employment of their loans.

That was the chief credit problem with the large government corporations. With private companies, the problems largely concerned the poor quality of foreign audits. Accounting practices overseas often differ considerably from those in the United States. Perhaps it is more accurate to say that they resemble U.S. accounting practices a hundred years ago. It is not uncommon in the Third World for a respected company to publish five different sets of financial statements which contain conflicting information. One set goes to the tax collector, one to the banks, one to the majority stockholders, one to the minority stockholders, and one to security analysts. In many countries, this is considered to be perfectly normal. As Price Waterhouse partner Joseph E. Connor observed, "In general, it can be said that . . . the accounting principles and reporting practices of many foreign countries . . . often have as their goal the furtherance of some national objective rather than being user, investor, or lender oriented as they are in the United States."

Thus all of the usual benchmarks were absent, and bankers like Rick Herrick were forced to rely more on instinct than they ever would with a domestic loan. But the instincts of American bankers in foreign countries, where they often lack fluency in the language, or, in the case of Herrick, are limited to one or two brief calls a year, are notoriously dull. More often than not they are at the mercy of the foreign auditors.

A recent example of this occurred in Taiwan where, since mid-1982, more than twenty-five large Taiwanese companies have defaulted on more than $500 million in loans. The general manager of Chase Manhattan in Taipei observed that many foreign banks were "fooled by the fact that [the statements] looked like American statements." Truth, in Third World accounting, is a fluid thing, more situational than absolute. By allowing three or five different sets of statements to circulate, the foreign country ensured that the banks would see only the rosiest of financial pictures.

When Herrick went before the loan committees, he was thus—in spite of his hard work—a virtual compendium of bad or questionable information, meticulously gathered and studiously analyzed. The bogus information network had performed splendidly: it had provided reams of data for Cleveland Trust's management to use in analyzing foreign credit, and it had answered every question anyone might care to ask about the state of a borrower's or country's finances. No one thought to question the system's fundamental accuracy. In the late seventies, that would have been an extreme form of heresy, tantamount to admitting that the half-trillion dollars that commercial banks had already loaned to the Third World had been lent on the basis of half-truths, errors, and lies. No one could afford to believe that, least of all the biggest commercial banks, who had disproportionately large exposures in the Third world, and who had the most to lose by scaring off smaller regionals like Cleveland Trust. I do not believe that anyone at Cleveland Trust understood the extent of the misinformation in the international credit system. They did not have the means or the knowledge to question it. That the bank's management was cautious about foreign lending—and relatively speaking it was—is entirely to its credit, although the reasons for this caution were far less explicit than those I have outlined in this chapter. Rick Herrick and his colleagues in Latin America were to increase Cleveland Trust's loan portfolio by some $100 million in Latin America in four years using this same process of information-gathering and analysis. The fact that the premise on which this lending was based was wrong was not fully apparent to Cleveland Trust until some $195 million of these Latin loans went bad in 1982 and 1983.

Chapter Four
THE INVISIBLE BANK

Il n'y a pas de solution. Donc, il n'y a pas de problème.

—MARCEL DUCHAMP

1

"WE'RE GOING to put you offshore in our Nassau branch for a few days, so you can see what a Eurodollar looks like. It's a fascinating little animal," my new boss, Charles Hammel, announced to me one day in late 1978.

Eleven months in the credit misinformation network had earned me the ninth floor, and I had just been promoted to what seemed to me the glorious and powerful rank of assistant international loan officer. The promotion had been carried off with a great deal of solemnity and punctilio—and they had installed me at one of those wide mahogany desks on the loan platform where I felt like a child in his father's chair. There was nothing on or in the desk except a small training manual, which explained in an overly simple way the large abstractions of the international banking system. All around me was the sound of voices on the phone, the sight of analysts dancing attendance on their loan officers, secretaries shuffling to and fro with correspondence, and occasionally someone dashing off with a look of desperate concern to the office of the division chief. I was about to begin my formal training, a three-month crash course in international lending. Soon I would be working for Charles Hammel, soliciting business in the Middle East and North Africa. "I want you to get the feel of how the Euromarkets work," Hammel continued, "because you'll be borrowing and lending a lot of money there. We run all that through Nassau."

I was surprised, thrilled; two days before I had been running off yards of calculator tape in the stultifying orange cubicles of the credit department. I had a brief vision of palm trees, warm trade winds, and a Caribbean town straight out of the Hollywood version of *To Have and Have Not.*

I asked him when I was to start.

"Now," he said with a smile. "Come on."

He led me across the platform and through a narrow door into the operations section of the international division, commonly known as the "Back Room." The Back Room was only a few feet beyond the wall where the Lichtenstein and Stella paintings hung, but as a social and working environment it could not have been more opposite. The loan platform was predominantly male, Protestant, and Anglo-Saxon; several of the officers belonged to Cleveland's old-line industrial families. Everywhere, there were pedigrees: boarding schools, famous universities, MBAs or advanced degrees in international affairs. The atmosphere in the front room was one of quiet, competitive gentility; the desks were clean and orderly, befitting the professional loan salesmen who occupied them. But coming through that door I realized that we had traversed several professional and social classes. The forty or so employees of the Back Room were far more typical of the average bank worker: predominantly female, black, and Hispanic, with usually nothing more than high-school degrees. They had a median salary of perhaps $12,000, while that of the officers on the platform was closer to $30,000. Their plain metal desks were crammed together, the walls barren. Everywhere was a litter of paper, files, stacks of documents, letters of credit, payments tickets, or accounting stubs.

This was the real bank in the more traditional sense: the Back Room moved the money, disbursed and kept track of loans, and handled all of the bank's documentary business. The work was tedious, unpleasant, the only compensation the vicarious experience of the foreign countries with which they dealt, the minor thrill of delivering twenty million dollars to some faceless corporate entity in Switzerland, Japan, or Egypt.

There was little opportunity to advance. In the clerical back rooms of Cleveland Trust, the most you could ordinarily hope for was a lateral transfer to a different but equally menial job just to break the monotony.

Through this crowded, prosaic environment Hammel led me back to an unoccupied desk wedged tightly against a standing partition. There were a few loose papers atop the desk and a set of rubber stamps and ink pads on one corner.

"This," he said, pointing, "is our Nassau Branch."

"I thought you were talking about the *real* Nassau," I said. "The Bahamas."

"I am," Hammel said. "From the point of view of the tax and regulatory authorities, this is the real Nassau. You should think of it that way. Everything you do here is 'offshore,' as though you were sitting on an island in the Atlantic. The money you move in and out of here stays offshore—forever, if we want it to. The fact that you aren't actually on an island isn't important. The whole thing is an abstraction, a legal and fiscal invention. That's all that matters. If the Fed and the IRS think this desk is sitting on an island in some Caribbean tax haven, then it is. They understand it. It's like pretending when you're a kid that your garage is a pirate ship. As long as everyone agrees to pretend it's a pirate ship, the system works. Have fun. Send me a postcard."

During the next week, I was introduced to the strange and marvelous phenomenon of "offshore banking," one of the darkest and most secretive areas of the international banking business. The stock-in-trade of the offshore bank was the Eurodollar, the stateless unit of value that is a monument to the inventive, abstract, illusionary things man can do with money, particularly when he is seeking refuge from government regulation. The Eurodollar was the denomination of most of the debt taken on by the Third World during the 1970s and 1980s. Its habitat, the Euromarket, was the single most important financial invention of the postwar world—a huge, unregulated, and demonically fast mechanism for raising billions of dollars of both long- and short-term loan capital and moving it across international borders. While the debt crisis was caused originally by the global transfer of wealth from rich nations to poor nations, it was the Euromarkets, specifically the Eurodollar itself, that facilitated it by enabling so much money to move so easily and so fast.

2

CLEVELAND TRUST'S Nassau branch—or what everyone was pretending was the Nassau branch—proved indeed to be a fascinating place. It was where Cleveland Trust bought and sold all of its Eurodollars. It held anywhere from $100 million to $500 million worth of them in loans and deposits. To preserve the fiction that these were Eurodollars and not regular old American dollars, I had to use a rubber stamp with a "Cleveland Trust Nassau Branch" logo on it to indicate the actual (pretend) origin of documents or payments. When I inquired why the Nassau branch itself did not perform this function (I still could not get rid of my Hollywood vision), I was told, with a patient smile, that for all practical purposes there was no such thing. There were no people in it, if that's what I was getting at. This was something of a shock, and it brought me up against a sticky conceptual problem: Where, spatially speaking, *were* those $500 million Eurodollars? They were not stuffed into the drawers of my imaginary Nassau branch, and there were no people or buildings or anything like that in the ostensibly real Nassau branch, and so there was no money there either. We were playing pretend with hundreds of millions of dollars. But this quality of pure illusion ended at the bottom line: the banking industry was making millions of dollars at this game. The Euromarket itself was bigger than the entire money supply of the United States. What did it all mean?

The first thing to know is that a Eurodollar is not a *physical* dollar. You cannot put one in your wallet. The Euromarket is cashless, its Eurodollars nothing more than electronic signals in the computers that keep track of the banks' deposit ledgers. The simple, accurate definition of a Eurodollar is that it is a U.S. dollar deposited in a bank outside the United States. Most are located in London, but there are Eurodollars in Hong Kong, Singapore, the Bahamas, the Caymans, Zurich, Luxembourg, or anywhere they are permitted to exist. The odd thing about them, though, is that in spite of the accuracy of this definition, all Eurodollars are really held within the United States.

This apparent paradox is perhaps best explained by the story of the creation of the first Eurodollar in 1949. That year, the Chinese Communist government decided that the U.S. government, for political reasons, was liable to "freeze" China's U.S. dollar deposits. (They were right: We did freeze what we could get our hands on in 1950, after the start of the Korean War.) The problem was that short of smuggling out millions of dollars in suitcases, which would in any case have been useless to transact official business, there was no way to keep dollar balances away from U.S. authorities. And of course they needed dollars, just like everyone else—no sane person would accept a renminbi in payment for anything outside of China. The solution was both clever and precedent-setting. The Chinese simply withdrew their dollars from U.S. banks and placed them in a Russian-owned bank in Paris called Banque Commerciale pour l'Europe du Nord, thereby creating an offshore deposit that was invisible to the U.S. banking authorities.

The method of the transaction explains the paradox. Prior to the transfer, the Chinese had what amounted to checking or savings accounts with U.S. banks—just like the kind you keep in your local bank—in the name of the Chinese government. Like your account, they were visible to the authorities, and therefore subject to freezing. The Chinese told their U.S. banks to move the funds from these accounts to a single large New York bank, with the instruction to credit them to the account of Banque Commerciale pour l'Europe du Nord. On receipt of the Chinese funds, Banque Commerciale then created a corresponding "Eurodollar" account in Paris—which was nothing more than a bookkeeping entry showing who owned the funds—at one remove from the New York dollars. As of the moment of the transfer, there was no longer any identifiable Chinese government account in the United States. The dollars were still in New York—but as far as U.S. banking authorities were concerned, they belonged to Banque Commerciale. The ultimate ownership of the dollars was perfectly disguised. The Chinese had full use of the money through the account in Paris. If they wanted to pay for imported oil, for example, they simply instructed Banque Commerciale to debit their account and transfer the funds to the oil exporter's account at another U.S. bank. The net effect of China's deposit at the New York bank was to create a dollar asset on the books of Banque Commerciale and a corresponding deposit liability to the Chinese government. The New York bank—and the Federal authorities—knew only that it had a deposit from Banque Commerciale. Eurodollars were thus created by the stroke of the bookkeeper's pen. They never left New York, but instead were layered at various removes from the original deposit.

In the process of making its dollar deposits invisible, however, a miraculous thing happened: the dollars slipped, as if by magic, into a stateless zone, where no sovereign authority had any power over them. They were officially on deposit with a French bank—but the French regulatory authorities were not concerned with dollars, which had no direct effect on their domestic money supply or credit levels. And the U.S. government could hardly control interest rates or credit levels of money that it could not see to quantify. If Banque Commerciale chose to lend that Chinese deposit to another European bank, the only record of the transaction within the United States would be a movement of money between accounts at the money center banks: there would be no evidence of any credit activity.

The Chinese proved that it was possible to disguise foreign-owned dollars held inside the United States. Soon after, the Russians began disguising their own deposits through both Banque Commerciale and Moscow Narodny Bank in London. This practice expanded with the growing tensions of the Cold War in the 1950s, and with the avowed willingness of the U.S. to freeze foreign deposits, as it did during the Suez Crisis of 1956.

The Suez Crisis was a landmark in the evolution of the Eurodollar for other reasons. It was then that after a century as the world's principal currency of exchange, the pound sterling was banned by the British as a medium to finance third-country trade. But the moribund banks of the declining British Empire quickly discovered that by setting up the same sort of offshore accounts, they themselves could finance third-country trade in dollars, and thus in the late 1950s an active but limited market for Eurodollars sprang up, with London as its center. The market tripled in size in 1959, then doubled again in 1960. And this was all going on under the noses of the British and American authorities, who neither comprehended what a Eurodollar was, nor had any idea of the extent of the market. As Euromarket expert Paul Einzig observed, "The Eurodollar market was for years hidden by a remarkable conspiracy of silence. . . . I stumbled on its existence by sheer accident in October 1959, and when I embarked on an enquiry about it in London banking circles several bankers emphatically asked me not to write about the new practice." The term "Eurodollar" itself did not appear in print until 1960.

The Eurodollar market—or more accurately the "Eurocurrencies" market, since it included a relatively small percentage of Euro-deutsche-marks, Euro-yen, and Euro-swiss francs—was born out of international distrust and the fear of expropriation and expanded when the British merchant banks found themselves shut off from their traditional bread-

and-butter business of financing foreign trade in pounds sterling. But in the 1960s, American banks found an even more ingenious use for the Eurodollar. Their move, en masse, into the Eurodollar was precipitated—quite unintentionally—by credit controls established by the U.S. government. Faced with the widening deficits created by the Vietnam War, the U.S. in 1966 and again in 1969 installed formidable "credit squeezes" which, among other things, limited the interest rate American banks could pay for deposits, including CDs. Because they were restricted from competing for deposit funds within the U.S., American banks looked to the Euromarket, where no such interest restrictions existed. By disguising their deposits—exactly the same way the Chinese had done—they could bid whatever they wanted for deposits from banks, corporations, and individuals, which they could then use to fund their loans to the booming U.S. multinationals.

Moreover, they could then take those deposits and lend them out without worrying about setting aside "reserve requirements," as they were required to do in the United States. This was one of the most appealing aspects of the Eurodollar, and it cut two ways. In the U.S., if a bank took a $1 million deposit from a customer, it was required by law to keep 3 percent—$30,000—in a non-interest-earning account at the Federal Reserve. That was dead money, earning nothing. But worse than that, from the banks' point of view, was a regulation limiting how much of the remaining $970,000 could be lent out to another customer. This reserve requirement varied between 10 and 20 percent. (The idea is that, if a bank lends out 100 percent of every dollar it takes in, it will have no cash left to cover the sort of bank run that has become commonplace during the last few years.) Assuming a 23 percent total reserve requirement, then, in the U.S. a bank could only lend out $770,000 of that $1 million. In short, the bank had to pay interest on the $1 million, but could only earn interest on the $770,000. A $1 million Eurodollar deposit, however, which carried no reserve requirement, could immediately be turned into a $1 million loan, and thus the bank could offer more competitive rates on loans and still make more money than it could playing by U.S. rules.

The new Euromarket thus offered many attractions. But in order to bid for Eurodollar deposits, U.S. banks had to establish offshore branches—and this resulted in what Stephen Mendelsohn called "the invasion of the world by American banks." Hundreds of banks rushed to establish branches in London and other Eurodollar havens to avoid the credit squeezes of 1966 and 1969 and to insure immunity from future squeezes.

The Euromarket was a banker's paradise: a world of the banks' own creation, with no laws, no regulators, and no central banks to interfere with the whims of the free market. It existed because it could offer rates higher than those of New York depositors; because it could move enormous quantities of both loan and arbitrage capital across borders with lightning speed and efficiency; and because it had become the focal point of the world's foreign exchange markets. By the early 1970s, "the City,"—the one-square-mile district in the heart of London that houses the Eurobanks—contained some 425 banking "vehicles" ranging from foreign consortium banks to representative offices of U.S. regionals.

As London grew so did smaller and more remote havens from credit controls and taxes. The most important of smaller havens in the 1960s and 1970s were the Bahamas and the Cayman Islands. In 1978, they held between them $100 billion Eurodollars, or roughly 11 percent of the gross Eurocurrency market. Nassau alone held approximately $75 billion. They had flourished because banks like Cleveland Trust were required by U.S. law to have an official offshore location if they were to deal in Eurodollars, and because all income earned by Nassau companies was tax-free. Cleveland Trust's "Nassau branch" consisted of nothing more than a brass plate on a building in Nassau, and an affiliation with a local lawyer, who had negotiated the initial registration fee and who held several nominal meetings a year on behalf of the bank. The lawyer conducted no official business on behalf of the bank but kept a nominal set of books, compiled and audited in Cleveland, in his file drawers. The lawyer performed the same function for hundreds of other U.S. banks and corporations.

How did Cleveland Trust create a Eurodollar? The process was simple. It worked exactly the same way the first Eurodeposit had worked for the Chinese. Only now, the offshore bank—the equivalent of Banque Commerciale—was a legal fiction known as the Nassau branch. And because Cleveland Trust was already a U.S. bank, it did not need the intermediary of a New York clearing bank. It simply transferred a domestic deposit from its books in Cleveland to a set of books labeled "Nassau," whereupon they took up offshore residence in the parallel universe of the Euromarket. That was all it took to disguise the original deposit—which might have come from East Cleveland—and to disguise all credit activity from the purview of the federal and state banking authorities. As long as the bank met the minimum requirements for an offshore branch, it could maintain the fiction that those Eurodollars were really there.

My job at the desk in the corner of Operations was really just house-keeping for the branch, making sure that everything was in its proper place, that Nassau documents all bore the logo of the offshore branch. The real Eurodollar action in the international division happened a hundred feet away, in a tiny, square room filled with Reuters screens, clocks showing the time of day in the world's major cities, and ticker-tape machines. This was the foreign exchange trading room, the domain of a smart, pleasantly eccentric vice-president named John Hansen. Hansen bought and sold all of the bank's Eurodollars and foreign exchange. Through his news wire, his telephone, and his Reuters screen he was hooked directly into the major trading markets of the world.

Hansen kept the official Nassau book, the record of all of the bank's transactions in Eurodollars. The way these transactions worked illus-trates why the Eurodollar market was such a useful invention. Let us say that a U.S. corporation—a client of Cleveland Trust—has a matur-ing Treasury bill, the proceeds of which have have landed in the cor-poration's account at Mellon Bank in Pittsburgh. The treasurer of the corporation now has $5 million sitting temporarily idle, and he will not need those funds for another thirty days. The treasurer is in the market for a short-term investment with a good yield. He notices in the *Wall Street Journal* that the rate for Eurodollar certificates of deposit is higher than that for American bank certificates of deposit. So he calls around to his banks asking for bids on a thirty-day Eurodollar deposit. He calls John Hansen, because his account officers at Cleveland Trust have pushed the idea that the bank can accommodate his needs for short-term off-shore investments. Hansen then calls around to various large American banks, shopping for a rate. The best he can get is 12 percent from Bank of America's Grand Cayman office, so he knocks an eighth of a point off that for CT's "spread," calls the treasurer back, and offers him 11⅞ percent for thirty days at Cleveland Trust's Nassau branch. The treas-urer takes it, and immediately transfers his $5 million to the account of the Nassau branch, thereby creating a Eurodollar deposit. Meanwhile, Hansen has already made his deal with Bank of America, and so he simultaneously transfers the money from his Nassau account to the ac-count of the bank's Grand Cayman branch. The entire transaction is accomplished in a few minutes. The corporate treasurer has fulfilled his desire to invest his money, Cleveland Trust has served its client, "matched" its book with a corresponding deposit, and made a small interest spread, and Bank of America has received a deposit at its Grand Cayman office.

But the money does not stop there. By placing that $5 million at Cleveland Trust's Nassau branch, the corporate treasurer has set off a staggering chain reaction that could send that money around the world several times in a single day. The possibilities are endless, and the sheer velocity of Eurodeposits frightening. Here is just one of an infinite number of possible combinations for that harmless-looking placement of excess cash: Upon receipt of the $5 million deposit from Cleveland Trust's Nassau branch, the Bank of America Grand Cayman places it instantly with Deutsche Bank's London branch, where because of its prime name it can command a better rate than Cleveland Trust, and thus earn a spread off the original deposit. Deutsche Bank London then relends it to Deutsche Bank's main office, which lends it to Volkswagen to pay for aluminum from Alcoa in Pittsburgh. Volkswagen transfers the proceeds of the loan to Alcoa's account at Mellon Bank. Thus the Eurodollars are "repatriated" to the same bank they started from, in as little as an hour. Because the funds have returned to onshore accounts, there is no surviving Eurodollar. But—here is the magic—Cleveland Trust's Nassau branch, Bank of America Grand Cayman, Deutsche Bank's London and main office branches all have $5 million Eurodollar assets (read: loans) on their books. So in aggregate $15 million additional Eurodollars have been created by the speed and electronic efficiency of the worldwide interbank lending network, on which the sun never sets. The whole transaction is highly hypothetical, because it assumes the integrity throughout of the $5 million, when in fact the amount of subsequent transfers would rarely match it. But the principle is the same. What happened essentially was that the original corporate deposit with Cleveland Trust Nassau became the funding for Volkswagen's purchase of aluminum. The difference is that instead of there being one intermediary, there were a host of them, and this was the nature of the Euromarket.

This was the most basic of Cleveland Trust's transactions in the Eurodollar market, and it was the principal reason for setting up its Nassau branch. But as the bank became more sophisticated, it began to fund its foreign loans in those markets. Its daily average of such borrowings rose steadily from $102 million in 1978 to $300 million in 1982, the year of the crisis. Its foreign placements of such deposits rose from $109 million to $350 million in the same period. And it was in this that the bank began to participate in a system of borrowing and lending which by its nature was to threaten the existence of America's major banks, and to virtually guarantee the insolvencies of Poland, Mexico, Brazil, Argentina, Venezuela, the Philippines, and dozens of other countries. For reasons which have become painfully apparent in the last two years, the Euromarket is an extremely dangerous place.

3

THE EUROMARKET grew by quantum leaps in the 1950s and 1960s in response to political events and to sovereign attempts to regulate credit. But the driving force was always the simple need of commercial banks to fund themselves—to obtain the use of money as cheaply and efficiently as possible to make corporate loans. Eurodeposits do not exist for their own sake; at the end of most of the deals is a trade transaction. Eurodollar finance is simply the grease that enables the international trade wheels to turn. The great lending boom of the seventies, which most experts date from Manufacturers Hanover's precedent-setting $80-million syndicated loan to Iran in 1969, was funded mainly by offshore deposits. But why did U.S. banks need the Euromarket? Why couldn't they simply fund their loans with their own domestic checking and savings accounts and corporate deposits? The pool of domestic funds was far more stable and certainly cheaper, at least in the days before the deregulation of interest rates, NOW accounts, and consumer money-market certificates (introduced in 1981). What explained the extraordinary boom, which would take the Euromarket in aggregate to an astonishing $2 trillion by 1984?

The answer is that the big U.S. banks had run out of domestic funds, as banks like Citicorp or Continental Illinois could not physically expand by branching into other areas, and thus could not compete in a national market for consumer deposits. They could of course solicit corporate deposits, but the intensity of the competition among the country's top hundred banks limited that source as well. How, then, were the banks to fund their geometrically expanding foreign loan portfolios in the 1970s? There was only one solution: Once they ran out of their traditional deposits, they had no choice but to buy the money on world markets from other banks. And the Euromarket in London offered what amounted to a huge financial supermarket for excess liquidity, free of reserve requirements and of all credit controls.

The practice of interbank lending in the Euromarket was the most radical and dangerous innovation in banking in the postwar world. It meant that instead of stable, traditional, and insured deposit bases, the big U.S. banks would be carrying as much as 50 percent of their liabilities in the form of large, volatile, short-term deposits from their fellow banks. According to Morgan Guaranty's estimates, some 70 percent of the Euromarket consists of interbank deposits. These deposits were known as "hot money" because they were extraordinarily sensitive to movements in interest rates. They were liable to move quickly in search of higher returns. But the term also connoted something far more ominous. This hot money was also free to flee at the first sign of trouble, which opened the door to the possibility of a wholesale "run" which could destroy a multibillion-dollar bank in a few days. Banks are far more fickle than either corporations or consumers—who are protected by the FDIC up to $100,000—particularly when the amounts involved are in the tens or hundreds of millions. A textbook example of the dangers of this hot money was offered in the summer of 1984 by the catastrophic run on the deposits of the Continental Illinois Bank and Trust Company of Chicago, a $45-billion bank, and the seventh largest in the nation.

Continental's home state of Illinois had traditionally maintained a "unit banking" rule which confined even its largest banks to one location. This was later liberalized to allow for two additional branches. Continental thus had the same basic problem that other American banks faced— diminishing returns—but to an extreme degree. Trapped by its branching laws, it began in the 1960s to buy more and more of its deposits from the money markets. This included borrowing from other banks and corporations in short-term money markets, selling certificates of deposit both in the U.S. and abroad (Eurodeposits), and selling its own commercial paper. Even then, its deposit mix carried an unusually high percentage of short-term hot money—against a very low ratio of stable consumer and corporate deposits.

In 1977, the bank began to expand its loan portfolios at such an extraordinary rate that it made even the New York bankers look sluggish. From 1977 to 1981 its domestic and foreign loan growth averaged 22 percent per year. At that rate its size would more than double every four years. Continental's international portfolio grew to nearly $10 billion, and it became known as the most aggressive and liberal of the domestic "energy" banks. Within a decade it had transformed itself into what its officers liked to call a "world class" bank, with lending strategies that, according to the *Wall Street Journal*, were "fed by a dangerous over-confidence, and an almost wild lack of control." The bad loans—some $4 billion of them by mid-1984—would come home to roost soon enough. But while business boomed, the bank's main problem was how to fund itself. Having reached the limits of its stable, lendable domestic funds, it was forced to seek overnight and thirty-day money to support its booming habit. Hot money was of course available within the United States, but Continental discovered—along with many other growth-crazy banks in the 1970s—that the Euromarket was by far the easiest, fastest, and most sympathetic system for raising that sort of money. The Euro-market, in fact, was designed with banks like Continental in mind, banks that needed vast amounts of short-term money to fund their long-term loans. The practice was known as "mismatching"—basically borrowing short and lending long—but it had never been done on this scale before. And so from 1977 to 1981, time deposits by foreign banks—Eurodollars for the most part—in Continental's foreign branches rose a stunning 91 percent to $12.8 billion, or nearly half of Continental's total deposits. (By contrast, even the aggressive Morgan Guaranty's deposits rose by only 71 percent.)

Continental was not the only bank building itself a financial house of cards in the Euromarkets. It was a participant, along with hundreds of other banks, in a frightening practice known as "leveraging." Leverage refers simply to that part of a bank's balance sheet not represented by capital. Banks had always leveraged to varying degrees; it is in the nature of banking for a bank to lend out more money than it has in stockholders' equity. A hypothetical bank with $10 million in capital and a good reputation can easily attract $90 million in deposits and then use this combination of funds to lend, say $75 million to customers, holding the rest in cash and securities. The leverage or "gearing" of this hypothetical bank is 10 to 1, the ratio of its assets to its capital. Leverage has always been a source of concern to bank regulators and economists. The reason is obvious: The less the assets of any financial system are underpinned by capital, the more it is at the mercy of a single large bankruptcy or panic. Imprudent leverage was one of the chief causes of the stock market crash in 1929; the thin margin requirements allowed investors, brokers, and investment trusts to borrow money against a minimum of stock collateral. And the more debt-inflated the system became, the more it was liable to the sort of jarring, whiplash contractions that ultimately destroyed it. So it is with the banking system. The less capital it has as a percentage of its assets, the less it is able to withstand adversity. In the United States in the twentieth century, a gearing ratio of 10 to 1 was considered a prudent upper limit, though the idea still horrified some people. Friederich Engels, for one, was morally offended to learn in 1892 that of the 28 million pounds sterling held by the fifteen largest banks in London, only 3 million pounds were actually available in cash. Yet there the leverage ratio was comfortably under 10 to 1.

But in the brave new world of hot money purchased in the Euromarkets of the 1970s, the notion of a prudent leverage had gone completely berserk. Ratios of 25 or 30 to 1 became commonplace. In Luxembourg, banking authorities considered an acceptable level of stockholder funds to be 3 percent of total assets, the equivalent of a 33 to 1 gearing. In Hong Kong, the standards were even more liberal and less defined. Even the Bank of England did not consider 30 to 1 to be inordinately high. In France, the government-owned banks like Banque Nationale de Paris and Société Générale sported ratios higher than 70 to 1. In the U.S., Continental's roughly 25 to 1 gearing was normal among the top ten banks.

But the real prodigy of the new leverage game was a new type of financial animal called a "Eurobank." The Eurobank was typically either a subsidiary of a large commercial bank or a "consortium"—a joint venture between two or more commercial banks. The first Eurobank was created in London in 1964, and by 1971 there were forty-six such entities. They were designed specifically to take advantage of the permissive rules on leverage and, more important, the fact that you could use that leverage to safely lend hundreds of billions of dollars to the developing world. All you needed was a track record in the banking business and a modest amount of capital to build yourself a large and profitable loan portfolio. The *modus operandi* of the Eurobank was simple. A large American or foreign bank would put up, say, $20 million—a tiny sum by modern standards that might represent 1 percent or less of the bank's total capital—and thereby create a Eurobank with an office in London. The new bank would then tap the interbank market, using its parent's reputation as collateral, in order to fund loans to foreign countries. The speed with which such a bank could assemble a loan portfolio was breathtaking. Within a few years it might easily have $600 million in assets (assuming a 30 to 1 gearing), most of which were in the form of participations in large international loans funded by 30- to 180-day deposits from fellow banks. The idea was to leverage the Eurobank as much as possible—at 30 to 1 you could afford to be viciously competitive in the international lending market, because even a small interest spread would mean a good return on such a small equity. There were no reserve requirements, no sovereign credit controls. Unlike its parents, which were at least subject to some domestic regulation in their home countries, the Eurobank operated in what amounted to a lawless environment.

The same climate of financial laxity and permissiveness that allowed the Eurobanks to flourish allowed Continental Illinois to leverage itself into a $45 billion bank. The problem, though, with pumping a financial institution up like that was that the hot money was liable to move quickly, and in great volume, at the first sign of trouble. A system leveraged at 20 to 30 to 1, built around billions of dollars of sovereign risk in the Third World, was an obvious candidate for the same whiplash contractions that occurred in the U.S. financial system in the early 1930s. But the financial community did not look at it that way. As a reward for Continental's arrogant, aggressive, and hazardous policies, it was named by *Dun's Review* in 1978 as one of the five best-managed U.S. companies. "Under the dynamic leadership of Chairman Roger E. Anderson," said *Dun's*, "Continental has garnered a reputation for quality service, innovation, and a pragmatic, rather than conservative, approach to banking." For its policies of imprudently leveraging itself with huge quantities of hot money, and on-lending it to Third World nations and high-risk oil ventures, Continental had come to be regarded by its peers as the model of a successful modern bank. The international banking system's biggest weakness, apparently, was its own inability to recognize danger. In May 1984 the same bankers and analysts who had lionized Continental since the mid-1970s helplessly watched the ruthless, wholesale destruction of the seventh largest bank in the U.S.

The immediate cause of Continental's problem was its deep involvement with a small Oklahoma bank called Penn Square. Penn Square had gone spectacularly bankrupt in July 1982, but not before it had sold Continental some $1 billion in oil loans, most of which turned out to be bad. Continental successfully camouflaged these problems for more than a year, but in the first quarter of 1984 the bank's results showed a shocking $400-million jump in "problem loans" to a record $2.3 billion. And it was in March 1984 that the drums started beating in both the Euromarket and the domestic money markets. As its operating losses mounted, both on its Penn Square loans and its $10-billion foreign portfolio, more and more depositors withdrew deposits, or kept them at deliberately short maturities. From the start, the jitteriest depositors of all were the foreign banks; and the least stable of all the bank's deposits were housed in its foreign branches.

The run on Continental's deposits began gradually, but by May 1984 rumors of the bank's impending failure were running like a firestorm through foreign markets. In one week in May, depositors yanked $9 billion of Continental's $28.3 billion in deposits. The run had started in Japan, led by the big Japanese banks—traditionally the most nervous of international creditors—had spread quickly to the big European banks, and then finally, sensing imminent disaster, U.S. banks and corporations fell into rank. In the sixty days from the first major run to the bank's bailout by the FDIC, it suffered a contraction of enormous proportions: It had lost $20 billion in net assets, fully $15 billion of which had been pulled by depositors, much of it from Continental's offshore branches.

By cutting and running at the first sign of trouble the Euromarket's participants proved what they had vehemently denied since the early 1970s: that a system of stateless hot money, free of sovereign controls, in which banks leverage themselves 30 to 1 in order to fund loan portfolios to Third World nations, was nothing more than a financial time bomb. The bankers had said all along that their leveraging was appropriate in the new age, that short-term deposits from foreigners were simply the new mode of funding, and that they were not inherently less stable than the old-style corporate and consumer funds. But their actions belied this. Such was the fear that even the FDIC's blanket guarantee of all depositors, great and small, could not stop the run on Continental Illinois.

The system's instability resulted from a combination of overreliance on short-term money and the building of large loan portfolios on top of tiny capital bases. The former gave vent to the fickleness of investment money, the latter supplied the crucial ingredients of fear and distrust. Continental Illinois was the victim of a system it had helped to create— and which had made it one of the most powerful banks in the world.

Nevertheless, the disastrous run on the bank is a minor incident compared with what would happen to the same markets if Argentina, Brazil, or Venezuela repudiated their debts. But the *principle* is exactly the same. All you need do is substitute Brazil and Argentina for Penn Square, and Citicorp, Bank of America, and Chase Manhattan for Continental Illinois. The money—especially the foreign money—would flee just as fast from their vaults as it fled from Continental's during the calamitous week in May when depositors pulled $9 billion.

4

IN WHAT must be regarded either as a stroke of brilliance or an accident of paranoid conservatism, Cleveland Trust itself was virtually immune to a funding crisis in the hot-money markets. Its chairman, Brock Weir, was something of a maverick in Cleveland banking circles, a Catholic Democrat from a California bank in a world of Episcopal Republicans from Shaker Heights and Gates Mills. He had taken the job at Cleveland Trust in 1972 and was responsible for the rapid growth of the international division. But when it came to the bottom line, he was still a rock-solid Cleveland banker in the old tradition. In 1978, the bank's 10.2 to 1 gearing was among the lowest for any large American bank. Weir was willing to lend abroad, even willing to fund himself in the Euromarkets, but he would never use the bank's $453 million in capital to leverage his assets. He would not take advantage of what was implicitly offered to all sound, multibillion-dollar American banks—the opportunity to double and double again in size in a decade, to do what Continental had done. It could have happened so easily. The telex machines buzzed all day long with offers of syndicated loans, the telephones in Hansen's office rang with funding offers. This turns out to have been a sound management decision. By keeping its gearing low, and by relying on the Euromarkets for less than 10 percent of its funding, Cleveland Trust could absorb large losses without encountering the sort of run Continental experienced. But this policy was the source of extreme bitterness and resentment among the international rank and file during the 1970s, who wanted nothing more than to be turned loose with their creativity and a large pile of money—just like Continental's and Citibank's officers were—to make that foreign loan portfolio really jump and earn a huge profit for the bank. It is to Weir's credit that he succeeded in reining in his quarterhorses on the ninth floor and kept his Euromarket funding at around $300 million.

But while the liability side of its balance sheet was safe from the vagaries of the Euromarket, the bank's asset side was not. This was because, willy-nilly, Cleveland Trust was participating in a system of foreign lending (loans are assets) which by its nature guaranteed the eventual default of the major borrowing countries. In the late 1960s, the banks came up with the idea of using variable or "floating" interest rates on their foreign loans.

The system was ingenious. The basic mechanism of Euromarket lending was mismatching: banks would borrow money in the form of 90- or 180-day deposits and lend the money to foreign companies or countries at longer terms. There was almost no way, under ordinary circumstances, to match a seven-year term loan with a corresponding seven-year deposit: In the protean money markets of the 1970s, especially after the oil crisis, fewer and fewer investors cared to risk their money that far into the future. What this meant was that in order to fund a loan, a commercial bank had to reborrow the funds twice or four times a year. This was called a "rollover." At each rollover, a new interest rate would be fixed. Thus, if a bank made a loan to Brazil at a fixed rate of 10 percent interest for seven years, it ran the risk that the cost of short-term money would rise above the loan's actual yield. If 180-day money was going for 20 percent, the bank would be seriously "underwater." Even the wildest of the foreign lenders would not have gone for a system like that. So in order to make it palatable it was decided that the borrowers—not the lenders—would bear all of the interest risk. The loans would be funded in the Euromarket at LIBOR—the London Interbank Offered Rate for short-term deposits—and would thereafter be pegged to whatever the LIBOR was at the time of the rollover. The banks' spread—the margin over LIBOR that would represent their interest income—would be fixed at the time of the loan. A seven-year loan to the Venezuelan oil monopoly Petroven might be made at "1½ percent over three-month LIBOR." If three-month LIBOR was 10 percent, the borrower would pay 11½ percent. If three-month LIBOR was 21 percent, it would pay 22½ percent. Either way, the banks got their cut.

For the banks, this was a miraculous way of sheltering themselves from the vicious interest cycles of the Western world. The world could go to hell, interest rates rocket through 25 percent, and their spread would still be built-in. In essence, they were not only sticking a borrower like the Philippines with $25 billion in debt, they were also leaving it at the mercy of the money markets in London and New York. The roughly 10 percent rise in interest rates that followed the second oil price increase in 1979 would mean $2.5 billion a year in additional interest payments alone for the Philippines. For a country like Brazil, with $90 billion in debt, the difference was a staggering $9 billion, all of which would have to be paid before Brazil could even consider repaying principal.

In seeking shelter from the interest cycles, Cleveland Trust was no exception. Interest rates floated on all of its foreign loans, usually over LIBOR, and occasionally over the U.S. prime rate. When it made medium-term loans to Société Nationale de Sidérurgie in Algeria or to a national telecommunications company in Korea, the bank was not only running the risk of the borrower itself. It had compounded the risk by adding a completely unknown factor to its loan equation: Neither Cleveland Trust nor any other bank could safely predict what the money markets would be doing even three months in advance. And this deeply undermined its credit analysis. In five years of banking with two rather different banks, I never once saw a risk analysis that took into account the remarkable dangers of domestic and Euromarket interest rates.

It was no wonder, then, that as rates rose through 20 percent in 1980, more and more international borrowing was going to pay interest on existing loans. This introduced the disturbing spectacle, which has become quite commonplace in the mid-1980s, of banks making loans whose purpose is to pay off interest owed to themselves. Interest goes to the bottom line, of course, but principal does not. So Citibank lends not to amortize principal, which would lighten the borrowers' burden; rather, it lends what amounts to interest payments owed itself, in order that its income statement continue to show a nice profit. All of which makes the bank's management and stockholders happy, but sinks the borrower deeper into debt. And this system of lending to one's own bottom line continued long after the worst months of the debt crisis, long after the illusion that principal would be repaid had died. For reasons known only to themselves, U.S. authorities continued to tolerate it. Many analysts feel that it was the interest rate hike after the second oil crisis that really put the Third World under in 1982 and 1983. Interest payments simply rose to a point where foreign countries could not borrow enough even to keep current, and when that happened, the illusion had to end.

Chapter Five

CAKEWALK

1

THE MOMENT could be taken from the lives and memories of a thousand international bankers. I am attending a reception at an expensive hotel in New York hosted by a Filipino bank which is anxious to advance its name in the capital markets of the Western Hemisphere. The bank has opened a New York branch and wants everyone to know about it. The way it does this is to spend a lot of money on food and liquor and a classy midtown venue, and to make sure that some of the local grandees show up. The Filipinos are good at this sort of thing, and they have put on a first-class soirée. There is unlimited liquor, which is brought around by liveried servants, and there is enough cold lobster and vintage wine on the tables to accommodate a party three times the size. All of this is important and has been so in the world of international banking since Rothschild hired Careme, one of the greatest chefs of the nineteenth century, to be his corporate cook. The symbolism is familiar to all in the banking fraternity: it is a language they all understand.

The reception is, to steal an oxymoron from Dr. Seuss, a wonderful, awful affair. The scene is loaded with irony. The Filipino bank is pretending to court the American banks, upon which the Philippines depends for its life blood. But in truth, the Filipino bank is a shy, wonderfully pretty debutante who has allowed all of her suitors to gather in one place. The illusion is carefully nurtured that for all appearances, the debutante is ugly and dull, desperate even for friendship. But the fact is that the bankers sampling the caviar and canapes are, in spite of their smiles and happy banter, dying to make LIBOR plus 1½ percent on a seven-year loan to the bank or one of its client companies. Plus commitment, management, and agency fees. This is what they are thinking. Those who have had too much to drink are thinking about what a wonderful life it is as an international banker, how comfortable and fun it is. But they are not doing their jobs.

What am *I* doing here? I am representing Cleveland Trust, and for the purposes of the reception I am a $5-billion bank, never mind that this is one of my first official trips, or that I am only twenty-five years old. Age does not matter much these days. Many of the people at the party are in their late twenties or early thirties and carry the rank of vice-president or senior vice-president. I am attending the reception because I am in New York on business, making calls on the local branches of foreign banks. New York on these terms is something I had only dreamed of before. I am staying at the Waldorf Astoria. I am free to call room service, without bothering the financial consciences of my senior management. If I want a thirty-five-dollar dinner, I can have it. But that is the low end, when I am by myself. For a business dinner there is technically no limit, and in fact I am *expected* to take my clients to expensive restaurants. I am also treated to meals. Today I was taken to lunch by the Bank of Tokyo, to a sushi bar near Wall Street where they picked up the tab for lunch: it came to eighty-five dollars for two. I make many calls in New York, during which I plead the trustworthiness and competence of my bank. I advertise the fact that we can lend $40 million to a single customer. I tell them that we are Ohio's largest bank, that we have many clients in common. I try to communicate what a nice, moderately aggressive, and trustworthy person I am.

What strikes me most about all this is the idea that I do not deserve it. I have really done nothing but sign on with a huge corporate organization which is permitted to leverage itself and sell its depositors' money in the remote corners of the world. When I am on the road, living the sort of life I could not possibly afford on a salary of $20,000 a year, I am living off the international banking system. At home I live in a lower-middle-class neighborhood on Cleveland's West Side. Here in New York or abroad I behave like the landed aristocracy. Why? There are two reasons.

The first is that we are selling what amounts to an abstraction. My company does not make goods, which I can sell on the basis of their superior quality or competitive cost. We do sell "services," which have to do with money management, but mainly we sell money itself, and everyone's money is the same. Most of the services are the same, too, at least among the larger banks. The "price" of money is also very nearly the same. We bankers seek, therefore, to find some sort of meaningful difference, where in fact there is none. This is why banks are so concerned with appearances; why especially a small international bank like Cleveland Trust must resolutely behave like it belongs in the big-time.

The second reason is an outcome of the miraculous microeconomics of banking in the new age. As I pointed out earlier, the cost-efficiency of foreign lending is staggering. It takes only one banker to solicit and put through a $20-million loan, which is a common enough figure these days. At 1½ percent over LIBOR, that means interest income of *$300,000 in the first year alone,* and as much as a million dollars over the life of the loan. Even if the international loan officer lives like a Vanderbilt, his job is still enormously cost-effective. And this only confirms the practice of luxury in the business.

But no one is talking business tonight. Bankers rarely do at these affairs, especially not in the company of competitors. The Filipino bank has trotted out its top brass and a few diplomatic types who spend most of the evening greeting senior officials from the American banks. There is an executive vice-president from Chase Manhattan, who wears his $80-billion corporate affiliation like an archbishop's chasuble. There are senior vice-presidents from all of the big New York, Chicago, and California banks, and they all move toward the three or four ranking Filipinos, attempting to make some meaningful contact without actually trying to sell anything. The rest of us supernumeraries scavenge around the corners of the party, chatting with the bank's assistant New York branch manager, or with managers of other foreign bank branches who have showed up for a free drink. The point is to look prosperous and be friendly. Posturing is everything.

There is an amusing historical precedent for this sort of posturing in a nineteenth-century American custom known as the "cakewalk." Mark Twain described it as follows:

> One at a time the contestants enter, clothed regardless of expense in what each considers the perfection of style and taste, and walk down the vacant central space and back again with that multitude of critical eyes on them. All that the competitor knows of fine airs and graces he throws into his carriage, all that he knows of seduc-

tive expression he throws into his countenance. He may use all the helps he can devise: watch chain to twirl with his fingers, cane to do graceful things with, a snowy handkerchief to flourish and get artful effects out of, shiny new stovepipe hat to assist in his courtly bows; and the colored lady may have a fan to work up *her* effects with, and smile over and blush behind, and she may add other helps according to her judgment.

Although the social milieu is quite different, the idea is exactly the same. In both the cakewalk, and the bank reception, the participants are pretending to be something they are not. Both are lies, but, to the people in attendance, very convincing ones. So much of the business works this way. Chase Manhattan's success in the 1970s was a direct result of its chairman David Rockefeller's overseas trips, which in sheer pomp and protocol make the Filipino bank reception look like kielbasa and bingo night at the local church. Rockefeller would rarely talk business on these trips. The idea was to roll out the corporate jet, the red carpet, and the magical name of American nobility, and to cakewalk the foreigner into doing business with Chase. This worked extremely well in places like Iran and Tunisia, where friendship with a monarch or potentate accomplished what hundreds of calls by lesser banks could not. Rockefeller had found an ingenious way to make a "meaningful difference" in a business where the product was both fungible and intangible.

This world of luxury was the banks' own invention, kept alive and healthy by the hundreds of billions of dollars in debt that were flowing overseas in those years. Its beneficiaries were the thousands of expendable, low-level, high-living operatives like me. International banking's headlong slide into foreign default would thus be a very comfortable one. It was difficult then to make the case that we were actually feeding off the poor people of the Third World. The link was tenuous, indirect. It would not be completely clear until the savage anti-IMF riots that took place in Latin America and the Caribbean in 1983 and 1984.

2

IN THE spring of 1979, I was in Geneva, Switzerland, with Charlie Hammel, en route to Algiers and my first encounter with the Third World. On a three-week trip, we would be calling in Algeria, Tunisia, Morocco, Bahrain, Kuwait, Abu Dhabi, Dubai, Saudi Arabia, and Israel.

We were at the Geneva airport, waiting for our Air Algérie flight, after having unwittingly made an illegal currency deal.

We had just come from the foreign exchange window of a Swiss bank, where we had exchanged a few hundred U.S. dollars for Algerian dinars. This was routine. Changing your dollars into local currency in advance meant that you could get out of the foreign airport that much quicker, because you had to pay for the taxicab in local currency. The man at the window had not batted an eye when we asked for dinars, and he gave us an extremely good rate. Pleased at our foresight, we boarded the Air Algérie 727 and took off for the Magreb.

On the plane, we happened to mention to another American banker the favorable rate of exchange we had gotten from the Swiss bank. He looked horrified.

"You mean you're *carrying* that stuff?" he whispered excitedly. "Now?"

We told him we were.

"Well you just made a black market deal, although you didn't know it. Those Swiss bastards don't care what happens, as long as they make a cut. The Algerian government doesn't allow the import of its own bank notes. If Algerian Customs finds the money they'll put you in jail. I'd stuff those in your shoes and pray you don't get the full rectal search."

So we stuffed and prayed and sweated all the way through Customs in Algiers airport. I was thus initiated into the shadowy world of "soft" currencies and foreign exchange controls, which would have such a powerful impact on the foreign debt situation a few years later.

A soft currency like the Algerian dinar is one that is not freely trade-able. That means that the Algerian government imposes strict controls on who may own a dinar deposit and who may not, and that the government, and the government alone, sets the rate at which the currency may be exchanged. Most of the world's currencies are like this. The only freely tradeable currencies—ones that you can hold, invest, and exchange for other currencies at will—are the U.S. dollar, the Canadian dollar, the deutsche mark, the Dutch gilder, the Swiss franc, the Hong Kong dollar, and the Saudi riyal.

Why do countries want to control their exchange rates? While the reason is complex, it is basically an attempt to stem what is considered to be a perverse speculative movement that is causing the value of the currency to drop precipitously against other currencies. Such speculation is triggered by the way merchants, investors, and ordinary individuals feel about the state of the economy's health—its inflation rate, productivity index, gross national product, foreign debt, political stability, and so forth. If the country's economy is perceived as weak, people will not want to hold its currency, and since currencies are like any other commodity, their value drops when demand weakens.

Now consider what happens if the Algerian dinar begins losing value against, say, the French franc, the currency of its major trading partner. Suddenly, a French product or commodity that cost four dinars in February costs six dinars in April. Then the price of nearly everything imported goes up. The more the dinar loses value, the more capital "flies" from it into stronger currencies, further depressing the rate of exchange, and further raising the cost of living. The one positive short-term effect is that Algeria's exports become more competitive on foreign markets. But the advantages of this to a country which imports far more than it exports are limited at best. For political reasons, such a situation is plainly against the government's interest. The easiest solution to the problem is to kill the market itself, by suspending trading in dinars, and by freezing the rate of exchange at a level acceptable to the general population. In countries with weak economies or economies that fluctuate considerably, there is often no other realistic political choice. With the exception of the U.S., whose dollar finances much of world trade, all of the other countries with hard currencies have, at one time or another, resorted to various controls in the last two decades. The effect of this is to create an artificial value for the currency—one that would never hold up under true market conditions.

We had broken the law at the Geneva airport because we had not purchased the Algerian bank notes from an official source. We had bought them on a parallel, competing, or "black" market where their value more closely approximated the actual value of the currency. In 1977, for example, one U.S. dollar bought 8.33 Algerian dinars on the black market, against 4.12 dinars at the official rate. We had bought our dinars at a rate somewhere between the two, but the transgression was the same. If the Algerian government tolerated such a market, its official rate would be meaningless.

Artificially valued currencies have much to do with the international debt crisis. In countries like Poland or Mexico, where the currency was fixed by the government at a rate three times stronger than the black market rate, much of their foreign debt went to subsidize foreign imports. You cannot prop up the value of a currency without in effect picking up the tab for the difference between the real and the official rates. When a peasant buys imported cooking oil, he is benefiting from the fact that the merchant who imported the oil was able to use artificially strong currency to pay for it. The peasant is paying perhaps ten pesos for what ought to cost thirty. The merchant is happy, the peasant is happy, but the government ends up paying for the false luxury of a strong currency. And the only way that the government was able to pay was through foreign loans. Many of the so-called sovereign "balance of payments" loans went to subsidize the most basic types of consumption. While this is very much in the short-term political interest of the country's leaders, it virtually assures that those loans will never be repaid, because the money was never invested in productive assets. One of the cardinal rules of credit is that you do not make a term loan to finance what amounts to working capital. Yet this is exactly what the banks did by lending to support current consumption.

Consumption subsidies also create vested interests among a country's monied classes. In Mexico, where there was both a fixed exchange rate and a law permitting the expatriation of currency (unlike Poland and Algeria), wealthy Mexicans benefited tremendously from the government-controlled peso/dollar exchange rate. They happily changed their inflated pesos for dollars, bought condominiums in the United States, and invested in the Euromarket. Here the subsidy begins to take on a more ominous look. The capital flight which occurred in Mexico in early 1982—and which effectively drained the country of much of its foreign exchange reserves—happened in anticipation of the government's official devaluation of the peso. Thus a large portion of the debt that flowed from American banks to Mexico ended up in the form of U.S. real estate purchases by anonymous Mexicans who did not have to repay a cent of it.

The banks had no control over this critical situation. They were of course all in favor of realistic currency rates in the Third World. The more realistic the rate, the less of their money was going to pay for unproductive subsidies. But as creditors they never required this; they never built any such agreements into their loan covenants, nor did they put any pressure on Third World governments. This was one of the reasons they later turned to the IMF, which specialized in forcing countries to devalue their currencies.

My little adventure between Geneva and Algiers illustrated one of the perversities of international lending which was chronically disregarded by commercial bankers as a source of trouble, and which resulted in billions of dollars in unproductive loans to the Third World.

3

RIDING THROUGH the outlying zones of Algiers, I was reminded of S. J. Perelman's observation that much of the urban Third World resembles the less attractive sections of Carteret, New Jersey. There are the same boxy, depressingly uniform rows of stucco flats and "dingbat" architecture that you find wherever you find postwar sprawl. But here the decay was extraordinary. Algiers, the capital and largest city of Algeria, was a monument to the inefficiency of bureaucratic socialism in the Third World. Everywhere there were mounds of garbage and debris, and rats and vermin roamed freely in the byways. Potable water was turned on for an average of one hour a day in most places in the city, and in more remote areas there was often no water available for days. Brownouts and power shortages occurred daily. If you were lucky, the telephones would work properly one out of five tries. Urban transportation was erratic and uncertain.

But these were only the outward signs of deeper social and economic problems. Algeria had one of the world's highest population growth rates. Since gaining independence from France in 1962 its population had doubled, creating the inevitable rural exodus to the coastal cities, which in turn caused a severe housing crisis. Thousands of homeless or quasi-homeless rural refugees were scattered through the city's streets.

In two decades, the state bureaucracy had nearly ruined the country's economy. Algeria's single productive asset was the result not of government planning but of a fortuitous geological accident: it possessed the world's fourth largest natural gas reserves and a million tons of crude oil. But instead of putting this to productive use, the government had taken the oil and gas revenues and had funneled them into a variety of inefficient, uncompetitive state-run enterprises. Hundreds of "political" factories ran at 30 percent of capacity and suffered massive worker absenteeism. The absenteeism was part of the chronic lack of foresight: the socialist planners had provided neither adequate housing nor adequate transportation for people to and from their places of work. In 1979, all state enterprises but one—Sonatrach, the oil monopoly—ran deficits.

But its industrial follies were nothing compared to the mess the government had made out of agriculture, the economy's traditional strength. At the time of its independence, Algeria was self-sufficient in food, and actually exporting wheat to foreign markets. By the time of my visit in 1979, Algeria was a net importer of a third of its cereals and 70 percent of its total food, at a cost of more than $1 billion a year. By abandoning agriculture in favor of heavy industries which did not work and made no money, Algeria had produced one of the worst examples of economic mismanagement by a Third World government in the postwar era.

And yet with all of its problems, and in spite of its track record of repeated failure, Algeria in 1979 was *one of the hottest borrowing countries in the world*. It ranked fourth as a recipient of private foreign loans and fifth overall on the World Debt Tables. Its foreign debt had risen from $2.9 billion in 1973 to more than $15 billion in 1979. Charlie Hammel and I had traveled thousands of miles from Cleveland to solicit loans here, because Algeria was, in the estimation of the world banking community, one of the three or four irresistible credit risks in the Third World.

It was thus an incredibly productive hunting ground for thousands of international bankers. The lobbies, restaurants, and coffee shops at the El Aurassi Hotel were full of them. We had all been drawn by the country's oil and gas reserves. A politically stable OPEC country that wanted to borrow heavily on the international loan market was simply too good to resist. It made little difference that the rest of its economy was falling apart, or that its government was allied with the Soviet Union, or that Algeria had been among the most militant OPEC members in advocating the increases in the price of oil. The government itself did not believe its own posturing. A joke that was current at the time has the president of Algeria coming to an intersection and being asked by the driver which direction to take. "What would President Carter do?" The answer: "He always turns right." "And what about Brezhnev?" "Always turns left." "In that case," the Algerian president replies, "put the blinker on left and turn right." They were happy to take advice, aid, and weapons from the Soviet Union, and equally happy to take billions of dollars from Western banks and to sell their natural gas to the highest bidder. For all of their inefficiency, they were a remarkably opportunistic people.

What mattered most to bankers, though, were those petroleum reserves, for they provided the critical answer to the chief question of all the credit committees back at the home office: Where are their export revenues going to come from so they can pay back our loan? As a loan officer, all you had to do was pull out those geologic tables. Algeria's huge liquified natural gas (LNG) contracts with the United States and France would provide the country with billions of dollars in foreign exchange through the year 2000. In the late 1970s, when Americans waited in gas lines and suffered double-digit inflation rates, oil was the magic word. You could see it in the volume of loans that were being pumped into the oil-producing nations: Iran, Mexico, Venezuela, Kuwait, the United Arab Emirates.

Hammel and I were staying at the El Aurassi Hotel, where all the foreign bankers stayed. It was a miserable hotel, and a perfect case study of what was wrong with Algeria. One of the less scrutable of the government's rules was that a restaurant could not fire a waiter, for any reason. This was abundantly apparent in the hotel restaurants, where surly, soup-stained waiters harassed the horrified foreign businessmen. The rooms had primitive heaters that did not work, telephones that worked infrequently, thick, brownish running water in the taps, and hot water every other night. If you ordered room service at 7 A.M., it would arrive with stone-cold food at 8:30. At the registration desk, the clerks often had no record of confirmed reservations, and the hotel's telex and telegraph service was notoriously unreliable. Still, it was by a wide margin the best hotel in Algiers.

In spite of this dirty, unpleasant ambiance, the place was jammed with foreign bankers and businessmen. They had descended on the oil and oil-service industries, and on the state industries which were fed by the oil money. We were no different. Hammel had been calling in Algiers for several years. In 1978 he had succeeded in making his first loan, a relatively prestigious participation in a syndicated loan to Société Nationale de Sidérurgie, the government steel company. Since almost all lending to Algeria was done by bank syndicates, we were there looking for more of the same. "Calling" in Algiers meant a ten-hour-a-day hunt through the state bureaucracies and multinational corporations for leads on participations in huge consortium loans. When we went to Sonatrach, the oil monopoly, we were not trying to sell them direct, standalone credits from the Cleveland Trust Company. Rather, we were trying to maneuver our way politically into someone else's loan. This was not unusual for a regional bank without foreign offices, nor was it unusual for a large money center bank that did not count itself among the hyperactive London syndicators. It was simply the way the game was played.

4

SYNDICATED LENDING was what international banking was really about in the 1970s and 1980s. Syndicates—which are simply groups of banks that band together to make large loans, usually under the leadership of one or two large banks—accounted for almost all of the sovereign lending from 1969 onward, and all of the loans that were made in excess of $350 million. The top six U.S. syndicators (Chase Manhattan, Citicorp, Bank of America, Morgan Guaranty, Manufacturers Hanover Trust, and Bankers Trust) together accounted for *$175 billion in foreign loans* between 1977 and 1982. Chase alone put together $46 billion, and Citicorp $45 billion. By any previous measure, the individual numbers were staggering. These six were not alone in the field, they were just the biggest. Most of the top twenty U.S. banks were involved as managers in some type of foreign syndication.

Syndication was in many ways the classic form of the cakewalk, because it was such a thoroughly public enterprise. Until the 1960s, banking, especially international banking, was a rather private affair. Discretion was the byword. But by the early 1970s banking had become much more competitive. In a banking world awash in excess liquidity, where hundreds of lenders were lined up in hopes of making loans to Algeria, Brazil, or Venezuela at cut-rate prices, the "meaningful difference" could no longer be communicated in private over lunch in the mahogany-wainscotted corporate dining room. The trend now was to go extremely public, to pay thousands of dollars to get your tombstones plastered over every financial journal from Hong Kong to Luxembourg; to proclaim to the world exactly how much money you were lending, and to whom, the idea being that you would get more business the bigger and more important you seemed. Investment banks had always done this, especially with public securities offerings, but there it made sense. The deal was public, after all, and it relied upon advertising to sell it to potential investors. With the loan syndicators, though, it was simply a matter of one-upping the Joneses. It was purely a matter of self-inflation.

Until 1968, there was no such thing as a syndicated Eurocurrency loan. Until 1969, when Manufacturers Hanover Limited, the first "Yankee'' merchant bank in London, organized an $80-million loan to Iran, there was no such thing as syndicated lending to the Third World. But the banks caught on fast. Their first big customers were U.S. corporations, whose credit had been restricted by foreign lending restraints imposed by the U.S. government. The lending horizon widened quickly. In 1972, the banks arranged 166 separate deals for new borrowers, including some for developing countries like Brazil and Mexico. The average size of a syndicated loan that year was $38.6 million, the average maturity 6.67 years, and the total of all syndicated loans was roughly $9 billion.

In 1973, the market entered its first boom cycle, which is still regarded by many as the high point of indiscriminate lending in the 1970s. The volume of syndicated loans more than doubled to $19.5 billion. The average deal doubled in size to $67.5 million, and the average maturity stretched to 8.6 years. The banks were offering terms that the amazed borrowers, who were used to receiving lectures from the big American and Canadian banks on the virtues of ''borrower discipline,'' would not have dreamed of asking for only two years before. That year the market saw unheard-of fifteen-year loans being made to the government of Brazil and to Pemex. Ten- and twelve-year maturities were being offered to such questionable developing countries as the Republic of Gabon, Zaire, and Nicaragua. And as the amounts rose and the maturities lengthened, a mysterious thing happened: the interest rates *dropped*. This ran dead against one of the oldest axioms of banking: the longer the loan, the higher the risk, and therefore the higher the interest rate. No one had ever seen a borrower's market quite like this one.

By the early 1970s, London was firmly established as the world center for all syndicated lending. The biggest players in the game were the offshore branches or merchant bank subsidiaries of U.S. commercial and investment banks, U.K. merchant and clearing banks, and large commercial banks from continental Europe, Canada, and Japan. (''Merchant banking'' is a Euromarket term nearly synonymous with ''investment banking'' in the United States.) They all had offices within the City, the financial district in London. They all employed professional syndicators, whose job was to put together individual loans as large as $2 billion involving hundreds of international banks. *Someone*, after all, had to take charge of moving all that money. Mere thirty-year-olds could claim in those days to have arranged a billion dollars a year in loans— virtually by themselves—from the First to the Third World. No one distrusted any of it yet; the fact that syndicated lending was untested by time made it that much more attractive. It was an innocent business in the early 1970s, and an entirely new form of commercial banking, though it had drawn for much of its expertise from the old international merchant banking nexus in London. London had been the world's banker for a century and a half; it housed the most powerful commercial banking network the world had ever known. And now, though the empire was sadly waning, its bankers still knew how to cut an international deal like no one else.

But how did these things get done? What was the process by which so much money moved so quickly and with so little thought of consequences? Syndicate loans usually originated with a call on the borrower by marketing officers of major commercial or investment banks—people very much like me, except that they worked for vastly larger and more powerful banks. Their jobs were to develop relationships with large potential borrowers, either through some sort of service such as deposit clearing, or simply by establishing a business friendship. They were essentially glad-handers, although they were generally smart and well versed in the rules of the game. This was the cakewalk par excellence: you made six or seven calls a year on a single borrower, took everyone with power or influence to an expensive meal, and tirelessly rehearsed for them the magnitude of your bank's assets, its track record in international lending, and its interest in helping the country to develop. You made sure that the senior management of your bank had a social weekend or two with the borrower's management. If you had done a good job, and your bank was powerful enough, one day a borrower such as Algeria might ask you—among others—to make a competitive bid on a proposed loan. This was where the real banking action began.

In a typical syndicate deal, several banks would bid against each other for what is known as a "mandate" to put together the loan. Once mandated, the bank became the lead manager in the loan, empowered to go out and solicit money from other banks. The lead manager's first task is to organize a "management group" to underwrite the entire loan. If the loan in question is for $500 million, the lead bank might underwrite $50 million itself, find six other banks willing to underwrite $50 million each, and another six banks willing to underwrite $25 million each. The former will become "managers" in the loan, the latter "co-managers." In exchange for agreeing to underwrite, the managers and co-managers will receive fees, though not as large as the *praecipuum* fee received by the lead manager, and the all-important prestige of being prominently displayed on the tombstone advertisement.

The management group thus contracts to underwrite the loan. The borrower is guaranteed that it will receive its money. It is now the managers' problem to ''sell down'' (get other banks) to take on their portions of the loan, the way an investment banker would sell off a stock issue it has underwritten—since they rarely want to get stuck with the full amount of their underwriting. In a $500-million loan, the managers might want to sell off as much as $300 million. So a meeting is arranged in London in which they sit around a boardroom table and draw up a list of hundreds of banks around the world they will solicit.

It is at this point that the rest of the financial community hears about the loan, as telexes begin whizzing around the various banks' international divisions. They contain ''offers'' to participate in the loan, up to a certain amount. The volume of such telexes at Cleveland Trust was astonishing in those years. It was common to arrive at the office and find a pile of ''bedsheet'' telexes covering my desk, offering millions of dollars in loan participations, all wanting quick replies. Many of the smaller international banks—particularly the consortium banks that operated out of London, Luxembourg, and Paris—did nothing but buy participations in these loans. They did not have to dispatch loan officers to hunt down foreign loans; they did not have to have a relationship with anyone save the managers in the deal. It mattered little to the big syndicating banks who the ''providers'' of funds were at the bottom end of a syndication. Their chief concern was to make sure that the loan was fully subscribed—a U.S. regional bank's money was as good as an Arab consortium's or a German clearing bank's. In some circles this was known as ''receptionist banking'': all you really needed in your banking office was someone to say yes to an offering telex.

The early 1970s saw a brand-new style of aggressive international banking in the form of competitive, cut-rate, syndicate lending. The speed with which loans were being arranged was breathtaking. In 1973 the mandated banks on large loans were often able to syndicate the entire deal in three or four days, so great was the appetite for foreign credit. According to syndications expert Robert P. McDonald of Chase Manhattan, ''Many of the participating banks had no firm understanding of whom they were lending to; very few performed any type of credit analysis and practically none had a tactical and/or strategic marketing plan delineated by geography." Volume was all that mattered. Many deals were rushed to completion—from mandate to signing—in less than three weeks. There was no precedent in history for the ability to raise that much money that fast. But it did not last.

The first boom cycle of the Eurocurrency lending market came to an abrupt halt in the summer of 1974. It ended with the bankruptcy of a small German bank called Bankhaus I.D. Herstatt, which owed several Euromarket banks millions of dollars. The Herstatt had been one of the most active banks in the Euromarket, in spite of its modest size. In fact, it was so aggressive that it had begun wildly, and illegally, speculating in foreign exchange, had suffered massive losses and concealed them by fixing its computerized books. On June 26, 1974, it owed $13 million to Morgan Guaranty, $12 million to Manufacturers Hanover, $10 million to Citicorp, $5 million to Bank of America, and $10 million to a British merchant bank called Hill Samuel. All of these transactions had been initiated that morning, before 10:30 A.M. New York time. They represented contracts for same-day delivery of foreign exchange, which meant that Herstatt had bought currencies from or sold them to the other banks. The American banks had delivered their side of the contract into Herstatt's accounts and, as of 10:30, were waiting for their money. These were routine transactions, and no one worried about them. Since the purchase and delivery were all to occur the same day, they were thought to carry no risk. But 10:30 A.M. New York time was 3:30 P.M. Frankfurt time—and that was the hour at which the German banking authorities moved to close the doors of Bankhaus I.D. Herstatt. The banks never got their money back.

The shock of Herstatt followed hard on the heels of the failure of Long Island's Franklin National Bank, America's twentieth largest bank, and the largest ever to fail. Franklin's sins were roughly the same: speculation and huge losses in foreign exchange. In February 1973, the U.S. dollar had been devalued a second time by 10 percent, which eroded confidence in the dollar-based Eurocurrency market. In October 1973, the Yom Kippur War had touched off the oil embargo and subsequent fourfold increase in the price of oil. All of this made investors nervous, but the Herstatt failure was more than the market could stand.

What Herstatt did was to cause the banks in the Euromarket to question—for the first time—the credit risk involved in interbank lending. And as soon as they permitted doubt to enter their minds, they suddenly saw a different world than they had perceived only a few weeks before.

The banking world was quite suddenly seen as an unstable, dangerous place. The effect was extraordinary. For over a month, only the strongest U.S. money center and foreign banks received interbank funds. What had happened was a crisis on the "liability" or funding side of the market. No sovereign bankruptcies had occurred yet and no one yet believed that they would—but now many of the banks that had made these loans could no longer fund them, or if they could find the funds, they had to pay premiums which put many of their cut-rate international loans "underwater"—meaning that they were now paying more for their deposits than they were earning on their loans.

By autumn 1974, a number of Eurobanks were either on the verge of disappearing or in a position of severe retrenchment. The basis of the entire Eurocurrency lending system was the assumption that the lending banks could always find cheap, easily accessible deposits, which would be automatically rolled over every three or six months, and were all based on a standard LIBOR rate. Now there were three or four tierings of that rate; now the bigger banks had cut back on lines of credit to smaller banks; now some banks could not find money at any price.

When international lending resumed that fall, borrowers found an entirely different set of rules than they had encountered just a few months before. The banks had been profoundly frightened by the funding crisis—astonished at how little it had taken to shake the system to its foundations. In a space of two months, their collective credit mentality had regressed four years, and the Eurocurrency market was again a lender's market. Borrowers could scarcely believe the new offers. The Polish bank Handlowy, for example, one of the more successful Euromarket borrowers, had borrowed four separate times early in 1974 at an average spread of ⅝ percent, and at maturities ranging from five to eight years. Now it was being offered no finer than 1⅜ percent, and no bank would consider a maturity longer than five years. Brazilian borrowers began the year borrowing at ¾ percent for twelve years, and ended the year at 1⅛ percent for five years. The entire market had tightened up, and lenders clearly called the terms.

Still, the new, disciplined lender's market lasted less than two years. In 1977 the market took off again on a new boom cycle that was to dwarf the sizable achievements of the first. The average spread that year was 1.29 percent, the deal size $74.4 million, the maturity six-and-a-half years. By 1979 the spread had crashed through the 1 percent barrier (the true signal of an emerging borrower's market) to .81, the average size for a single loan had grown to $100 million, and the maturities had been stretched back out to eight years. And the price competition was such that fully a third of the new loans were going to refinance existing loans at cheaper rates. By 1979, borrower-lender loyalty was a thing of the past. Now all that mattered was price, and the bank with the cheapest rate invariably got the mandate.

Cleveland Trust's first loan to Algeria was a $2-million participation in a $13.7-million syndicated loan. This is a tiny loan by Euromarket standards, but it worked the same way the big ones did, with all of the same hazards. The way Hammel had hunted it down, sold it, and driven it through the bank's credit commitees was typical of the *modus operandi* of many regional banks in the 1970s and 1980s: he went through an American client.

The client in this case was an international construction and contracting firm called Bechtel, based in San Francisco. Bechtel was a Fortune 500 company, a "prime" name, and a major target company of Cleveland Trust's national division, which employed two loan officers to cover the West Coast. Bechtel's treasury people in San Francisco had told the Cleveland Trust officers that the way to get a piece of Bechtel's domestic business was by assisting its overseas sales.

Bechtel had large operations in Algeria. Hammel had called on their local office many times, taking the long taxi ride out of Algiers to Bechtel's plush, colonial, tile-mosaic villa in the suburbs; he was looking for leads. The purpose of his calling was to find out what sort of business Bechtel was doing in Algeria and which state corporations were buying it. After a number of calls, he finally found one in early 1978. Bechtel had contracted to provide blueprints for a new cold-rolled steel mill for Société Nationale de Sidérurgie. To pay for the blueprints, SNS needed foreign money. So Hammel paid a call on SNS. What he found out, eventually, was that the Los Angeles-based United California Bank had been given the mandate to put together a small, $13.7-million syndicate. It was a "restricted" mandate—SNS and Bechtel would tell UCB what banks it would and would not invite in the interest of broadening their pool of friendly banks. For Hammel, this stage of the banking process had become a political maneuver: he had secured the support of the national division for a loan to SNS in support of Bechtel, which meant that, at the critical moment in a committee meeting, a senior vice-president from the national division would speak in favor of the loan. He had then convinced Bechtel's people in Algeria to support Cleveland Trust's participation in the loan. Finally, with the help of Bechtel, he had persuaded the borrower itself to ask UCB to invite Cleveland Trust into the loan.

The formal invitation to join the loan had arrived in the form of a telex from United California Bank. It carried the terms of the deal, rates, fees, and who would guarantee it. Hammel then wrote a country study for Algeria, along with an analysis of the financial figures of both the borrower and the guarantor—the government-owned Banque Extérieure d'Algérie. It was approved as presented by Cleveland Trust's senior loan committee.

It was a typical international deal. The bank had not solicited the original loan, had done very little credit work on its own. It had never made a loan in Algeria before. It had simply signed on—through the diligence of Charles Hammel—to someone else's deal. The participants in the loan included three other regionals (presumably there for the same reasons as Cleveland Trust), two Japanese banks, an Arab consortium bank, the Royal Bank of Scotland, and a Hong Kong merchant bank. They were all parties to a cumbersome loan agreement that had been worked out by UCB's legal staff, the purpose of which was primarily to protect the lenders. In fact, this agreement, and most of the agreements supporting the large loans made from 1968 on, accomplished nothing of the sort. It offered almost no creditor protection at all, and in truth existed merely to assuage the financial consciences of the bankers involved.

5

As WAS illustrated earlier, the credit analysis that underpinned most sovereign lending was long on wishful thinking and terribly short on hard facts or prudent banking. The banks' lack of control over a country's aggregate debt, combined with the awesome money-moving power of the syndicated loan, virtually guaranteed that many of those loans would never be paid back. The premises were all wrong. But there is yet another absurdity to pile on top of the already high pile: given that the loans were doomed, at least in the near term, one might have thought that the banks would be able to recoup some of their money, the way they would if you were unfortunate enough to miss a few car payments or mortgage installments. But the banks' painstakingly constructed loan agreements, full of language about default and its consequences, were utterly useless in the face of sovereign failure to pay off debt.

A country cannot go bankrupt. This fact is often cited by bankers as a good reason to continue lending money to them. In fact, just the opposite is true. If a country cannot go bankrupt, it means that you cannot force it into liquidation, and if you cannot force it into liquidation, you cannot sell its assets in order to pay off your loan. If Brazil had been a U.S. corporation that owed $93 billion, the lending syndicate would almost certainly have declared an event of default and moved to the courts for redress. In banking this is known as "recourse." The company would have been dismantled, sold, and the banks would have recouped as many cents on the dollar as they could reasonably get. If they were well secured, they might even get most of their money back. But if a bank cannot hold the threat of liquidation over the borrower's head, then it can threaten him with nothing at all save cessation of new credit. A loan agreement is supposed to provide creditors with a predictable, orderly way of handling an event of default. The agreements underlying the big syndicate loans did not.

The first real test of the sovereign, syndicated loan agreement came in 1979 with the coercive default of Iran, and it failed miserably. When Iranian President Bani-Sadr announced that Iran would withdraw its deposits from U.S. banks, the banks panicked and persuaded Jimmy Carter to freeze Iranian assets held in the U.S. Freezing their dollar accounts, of course, made it impossible for the Iranians to make payment on their debt. And so Chase Manhattan immediately declared a default and "accelerated" the maturity of the loans it had made on its own and in several large syndicates. This triggered cross-default clauses in everyone else's loan agreements with Iran, which then triggered a mad scramble for pieces of those frozen assets. The resolution of the problem should have been dictated automatically by the loan agreements the banks had with Iran and with each other in their syndicates. In fact, though, the banks quickly learned that none of their agreements, alone or together, could serve as even a general guide for action, much less serve to settle disputes. There were too many banks, too many syndicates, too many cross-default clauses for any single loan agreement to have the slightest effect. The complex legal process that followed, which Walter Wriston suggested would comfortably support several generations of lawyers, involved twenty-six loans (most of them syndicated), more than a hundred and fifty lenders, and took fifteen months to settle. The settlement made only occasional and passing reference to the underlying loan documentation. In the final analysis, their clauses, covenants, and "events of default" had no legal merit.

So the banks' elaborate loan agreements had provided no help at all— even though, in the case of Iran, the money to repay the loans was readily at hand. it would be difficult to imagine the depth of confusion if the same thing occurred in Brazil, Mexico, or the Philippines, which have few assets in the U.S. and relatively huge debt exposures.

To understand why the banks found themselves cornered and forced to "reschedule" debt, imagine for a moment that you are a large bank, like Morgan Guaranty. You have syndicated billions of dollars in loans to Brazil. Brazil's finance minister tells you one day that the country cannot pay you back—not now, and perhaps not for a long time. Principal and interest payments stop coming. According to your loan agreement, you now have what is called an "event of default." This gives you the legal right to "accelerate maturity," i.e., to make the full amount of the loan immediately due and payable. So let's say that you, Morgan Guaranty, as a responsible, prudent bank, go ahead and do just that. You say, "Brazil, pay up, or else."

The immediate implication of calling the loan is that you will trigger every cross-default clause in every loan anyone has ever made to Brazil. This will account for most of the country's $93 billion in debt. A cross-default clause is a kind of doomsday device: it says that if the borrower is in default on any single loan, then he is in default on all loans. Because of this provision, all creditors put themselves on an equal footing with each other. It insures that all banks would have to be cooperative when the time came and agree to reschedule the loans on the same terms—the alternative being nothing less than financial Armageddon.

Now that you have created a world panic by accelerating Brazil's loans, you can start to think about how you are going to force the country to pay you back, even though it has no foreign exchange reserves. This is an interesting concept which goes right to the heart of the debt crisis. It explains why banks since 1982 have gone along with the rescheduling of every loan they ever made to countries that cannot repay them. The point is this: you have no recourse. You may threaten to seal a borrower up in a creditless darkness, you may threaten to seize every asset it owns overseas—its securities, its bank accounts, its airliners, tankers, and even the furniture in its embassies—but then of course you remove what remains of the borrower's incentive to repay. It is a no-win situation.

As an international loan officer, I was essentially a salesman. Accordingly, in my accelerated training program, heavy emphasis was placed on "marketing." In the competitive marketplace, where thousands of banks were pushing loans overseas, you had to be a good salesman. But while I learned how to sell and disburse loans, I was taught very little about how to collect them if they went bad. Few of us had any idea of either the risk we were taking, or of the staggering difficulty we would face in getting our money back if our borrowers defaulted. Bad loans are an unavoidable part of banking, which is, after all, a risk business. But I knew very few international lenders who had ever handled a bad loan overseas prior to 1982. There was an antiseptic quality about the whole process, and we simply never figured that we would have to go out and get that money back. Sustaining this illusion was the unspoken conviction that the debt was just too big, the countries too crucial to U.S. global politics, and the banks too important to our economy to allow a major sovereign default to occur.

Consider Cleveland Trust's loan to SNS, which I was charged with monitoring. As a banker I was trained to be sensitive to my "security," real or imagined, in the loans I made. Our security on the loan was a guarantee from the Banque Extérieure d'Algérie, one of the big government banks. As Hammel and I walked into our call at SNS, I found myself wondering just what it would mean if SNS became insolvent, unable to get its factories up and working. But that situation already existed, I reminded myself. SNS was a losing proposition, kept alive by rechanneled oil revenues from Sonatrach. A government corporation that was losing money was thus being guaranteed by a government bank that was on the same gravy train. So the loan to the company and the guarantee of that loan were only as good as the country of Algeria, whose overall borrowing habits we could not control, and whose political and economic fate was unknown. Our loan was therefore unsecured in any traditional sense of the word. SNS would never default as long as Algeria was solvent, and if Algeria was solvent, then BEA was solvent. It was a neat, symmetrical arrangement; yet this was bona fide sovereign risk.

In the U.S. a loan to a steel mill would be secured ultimately by the assets of the mill itself. We would have legal right of "offset" against the company's bank accounts. We could persuade the courts to seize its physical assets. It was my job as a loan officer to keep track of the borrower's financial condition, to look for early-warning signs that might indicate an inability to pay off the loan. But with our loan to SNS, it scarcely mattered whether I kept track of the financial condition of SNS, BEA, or even of Algeria itself, *because there was nothing I could do about it anyway*. A default by one would imply a default by all three, and if that happened, Cleveland Trust with its paltry $2 million was hardly in a position to dictate terms to anyone. If Algeria ran out of money, our loan agreement with its guarantee would be useless, as would all loan agreements made by all big bank syndicates. Unable to force Algeria to liquidate assets, the banks would do what they always did in a crisis: get together in New York or London and work out a rescheduling of some sort.

This is exactly what has been happening in Latin America in the 1980s, proving the uselessness of the syndicate loan agreements in protecting the banks' interests. Some $350 billion in loans have been rescheduled since August 1982, representing dozens of separate crises, to which the banks' response has always been the same: They will agree to anything, because they have no choice. Argentina was the first to call the banks' bluff, the first to discover just how powerless they really were, for all their bluster and bravado. Argentina held out for a period of months in 1984, refusing to cooperate with either the IMF or the banks, disregarding the vague and unsupportable threat of "cessation of credit" that the banks dangled before it. Predictably, Argentina got its way—in fact, it could have dictated any terms it wanted. Argentina could do this because the consequences of straight-out default would be unbearable for banks like Citicorp, Bank of America, and Manufacturers Hanover. In sovereign lending, the borrower holds the whip, and this has been a painful discovery for the banks.

Algeria itself never got into any real trouble. It was one of the few countries in the world that was smart enough to exercise any borrower discipline. It could have borrowed billions more than it did. This was a remarkable achievement in the early 1980s, when getting rid of aggressive bankers was, as Lincoln said of bureaucrats, like trying to shovel fleas off your barn floor. But that, for Cleveland Trust, is merely a stroke of good luck, not a result of prudent banking. Had Algeria decided to borrow $30 billion more, there was nothing in our syndicate loan agreement with United California Bank to prevent it from doing so. There would have been no way to call in our loan, or to seize physical or financial assets. The bank was lucky in Algeria, and unlucky in Brazil, Mexico, and Venezuela. In all cases, it had no control over the fate of its loans.

Chapter Six:

A ROVING COMMISSION

1

PEDDLING LOANS for a regional bank in the Arab countries of the Middle East and North Africa is like walking through an Arab souk: you never know quite where you are, or quite what you are looking for. Out in the streets of Jeddah, Saudi Arabia, where the temperature is hitting 118 degrees at midday, and where the glistening, Miesian skyscrapers provide shade for tribal bedouins, this notion comes home hard. I am in a foreign land, one that I visit only twice a year, and then only for a few days. I neither speak the language, nor understand the customs, knowing only what I have read in magazines and what I can observe on the streets. I have been sent to Saudi Arabia to expand Cleveland Trust's loan portfolio, and to attract foreign deposits to the bank's domestic and offshore branches. I cannot help imagining what some resident of Cleveland's West Side, whose deposits I am trying to lend here, would think about all this. I imagine a working-class fellow transported from his job on the Ford assembly line to the middle of Jeddah on a June day, and I'm trying to explain to him why it is important that we lend his deposit here. The idea is funny, and the reason it is funny is because of the obviously large gulf between the domestic depositor and the international bank.

In spite of the country's huge oil revenues, there is plenty of lending business here among the private-sector trading companies, the banks, and the foreign multinationals. And Saudi Arabia is the source of more foreign deposits than any other developing country on earth. The problem is how to get at that business from a base 5,000 miles away, especially with packs of foreign bankers roaming the superheated, garbage-strewn streets. So I am out in this heat making six or seven calls a day. It is not an easy job, and it is not glamorous. Almost no one has ever heard of Cleveland Trust in Saudi Arabia, and much of my time is spent explaining to amazed target customers just exactly why this little Ohio bank is out poking about in the Middle East. I have made calls in dark, filthy little offices because I had pulled the name of a local licensee for some domestic customer's product off a list somewhere, only to find a company that has not sold a foreign product in years. I have called on bankers in plush offices who honestly cannot figure out what it is I want to do for them, and who serve coffee and chat politely in confusion until the end of the call. I have encountered foreigners who are desperate to have a loan under any pretext. And I have also made calls on friendly Americans who work for client subsidiaries who are delighted to see another American, and who are anxious to do business. The latter type is the rarest of the lot, and by far the most profitable. What my superiors would like to believe I am doing is looking for leads on trade finance—loans that will support our domestic customers' sales. That is the name of the game at Cleveland Trust. To a lesser degree, I am encouraged also to call on banks, too, because it is important to know the people who move the money, and because Cleveland Trust's loan committees like that sort of business in moderate doses.

Both traveling and lending here are risky, and most of the risk originates somewhere in the Koran, which seems to govern all aspects of Saudi life. For example, if the taxicab I am riding in has an accident, the Koran says that I am personally liable for all damages, injuries, or loss of life, on the theory that the driver would not have been there to have the accident if I had not hired him. I have been told to flee the taxi if this happens and lose myself, in my pinstripe suit, in the souks. It is a daunting prospect.

The evidence of religion is everywhere, from the sight of thousands of Saudis—including my clients—spreading their prayer mats out and praying toward Mecca five times a day, to the little reminders in my guidebooks that I can be jailed for possession of alcohol, to the laws against charging interest on loans, which the Saudi banks cleverly sidestep. The Saudis do not take kindly to foreign interlopers who disregard their rules of conduct. The day before my arrival, an Air France stewardess had gone topless at the Meridien Hotel's swimming pool. There was a panic for a few hours, the woman was banished forever, and by the time I got there, men and women had been segregated at the pool by hours of the day.

There is absolutely no way to keep track of the country's religious climate from Cleveland. An underdeveloped and devoutly Islamic country has been propelled with awesome speed into the age of computers, high-rise buildings, and telecommunications systems. Everywhere, there is a collision of modern and premodern society. Women who are not allowed to drive cars or even to attend mosques can now observe foreign women in short skirts, and Air France stewardesses behaving in a way that most of the noncosmopolitan world would consider grossly immoral. The large oil revenues have created a class of jet-setters atop the society, sheiks who own houses in Switzerland or Miami, and who like to drink and have parties and go to R-rated movies, all of which are punishable offenses in Saudi Arabia. Western businessmen tell of Saudi princesses wearing miniskirts under their dish-dashas and purdah, hopping off planes in Paris and heading straight for the discotheques. And none of this sits very well with the folks back home. There is an antimodern strain in Islam that showed itself in Iran with the rise to power of the Ayatollah Khomeini. There are outbursts of it from time to time in Saudi Arabia—such as the armed occupation of the mosque in Mecca—most of which are not covered by the Western press. But there is almost no way Charles Hammel and I can track it with our semiannual visits, just as there was no way we could track it in Iran, where we got stuck with a liability on a letter of credit after the revolution. We would be the last to know if a religious revolution swept Saudi Arabia. We would be able to do nothing, as we had been able to do nothing in Iran, to protect our interests. Out on the streets of Jeddah, or Riyadh, or Dhahran, this is painfully obvious. At bottom, this is a crap shoot, a bet that what happened in Iran will not happen here. If there is a religious revolt in Saudi Arabia, all we can do is watch and hope that whatever government emerges will be sympathetic to Western banks.

Charles Hammel had a difficult time of it squeezing business out of Saudi Arabia. In seven years he managed to develop only a handful of customers, in spite of the fact that he is very good at what he does and is remarkably persistent. After traveling there several times, both with Hammel and alone, I concluded that that was very nearly the best we would ever do. Each bank had been alotted its share; our was perfectly in keeping with our size and influence. We had a $6.25-million line of credit out to a sprawling company called E. A. Juffali Brothers. Juffali has the distinction of being the Mercedes dealer for all of Saudi Arabia, a brilliant concession in that country. Juffali also sells Kelvinator refrigerators. Kelvinator is a domestic client of Cleveland Trust and provided the original lead to this business. We financed what is known as "floor planning"—a period of three to six months during which Juffali would sell the refrigerators off its showroom floors. We also provided a financial guarantee on behalf of a client called Diebold, which was constructing the safe in which the Saudi Arabian Monetary Fund, with $55 billion in foreign assets, would keep cash and securities. We had a few lines of credit out to Saudi banks, but they were rarely used. The sum total of annual business that Hammel had been able to develop there in seven years was less than $10 million.

Still, this was Hammel's chosen domain, and he liked the work. The profound sense of alienation that I felt did not seem to bother him in the least. To him, "snipe hunting," as he called it, was simply the fate of the officers of a $5-billion regional bank with no foreign offices. He had been knocking on thousands of doors in the region for seven years: in Tunis, Algiers, Casablanca, Rabat, Kuwait City, Abu Dhabi, Dubai, Jeddah, Riyadh, Dhahran, Bahrain, Damascus, Beirut, Tehran, even Muscat. His attitude was amused, cynical, and full of the conviction that humor was the only proper response to the vicissitudes of life as an international money peddler: You did your best, and you took what you got. His total outstanding loans and credits in the Arab countries rarely exceeded $15 million. By regional bank standards, this was perhaps an average portfolio.

But Hammel's real achievement in the Middle East—and what really allowed him to tolerate the dead-slow business in the Arab countries— was his loan portfolio in Israel, where he had elevated Cleveland Trust to among the top American banks by outstanding loans. In his younger days, he had been a member of a blue-ribbon international commission sent to study Israel's economy. Now he had over $40 million in outstanding loans there and commitments to lend more. In Israel, everyone in the financial world knew who he was.

Hammel's total portfolio in the region amounted to some $60 million, with unused lines of credit amounting to perhaps another $15 or $20 million. I catalogue this in order to point out the unheralded role of the regional bank in international finance. The type of portfolio Hammel had put together over the years was not unique to Cleveland Trust. There were hundreds more like us out there, banks with few or no foreign branches. Individually, we had the same sort of anonymous loan portfolios that would attract no attention anywhere. We each, as the Fuller brushmen of the international banking business, had carved out a tiny area of specialization. Most of the regionals did not have any branches in the Middle East, and because our loan volume was small, we were not "market makers" in any sense of the term. But *collectively* we were lending vast sums of money overseas. Like most of these banks, Cleveland Trust followed the market and played by rules that were being continually rewritten by bigger banks. They decided which countries were the good borrowers; they set the rates and the terms; they pioneered all of the lending techniques that the rest of us would later use. For us it was a form of scavenging: the overwhelming market share, including the big, fee-laden loans, went to the giant international banks. We picked up the leavings—small participations in syndicate loans, assorted short-term credits to foreign banks, or the occasional client-related trade finance deal that had somehow been overlooked by the canvassing efforts of the big banks. Since so many of the world's prime borrowers were heavily visited—at Sonatrach in Algiers, for example, I was the fortieth foreign banker in less than three weeks to sign their guestbook—business was something to be stumbled upon by accident, and even if you found it, there was no guarantee that you could sell it to the committees back home.

Compared to the bankers at Citibank or Bank of America, Hammel was a bit like Dashiell Hammett's Continental Op: tough, resourceful, usually alone, and with small resources behind him. There were thousands of Hammels abroad in the late 1970s, gliding anonymously from place to place in the Third World, trying to sell the services of small- or medium-sized banks.

Their counterparts from the money centers tended to regard the regional bankers with mild annoyance. And they were not above cranking themselves up to full, $75-billion arrogance when you spoke with them. After all, Cleveland Trust was putting out a few million here and there, while they were moving billions, taking in huge deposits, and introducing the foreign countries to many of the types of financing that we were out there trying to sell.

But for all of the righteous arrogance of the big-time bankers, the regionals and smaller money center banks were in fact the real foot soldiers of the international lending system. The big banks made the news when they arranged a large loan, or when a large loan went bad. It was far more sensational to say that Bank of America had loaned $2.5 billion—50 percent of its capital—to Brazil than to say that First Wisconsin had loaned $70 million—22 percent of its capital—to Argentina. But the regionals provided much of the money that went from America to the rest of the world. As of 1984, foreign borrowers owed roughly $350 billion to American banks. A huge chunk of that—some $120 billion—was owed to the top five banks alone, the ones you read about in the newspapers. That leaves $230 billion owed to other banks. Of this amount, some $80 billion was owed to the remainder of the top fifteen banks, all but two of which were located in money centers. That still leaves $150 billion owed to smaller banks—roughly 43 percent of all debt owed to U.S. banks from overseas. The great debt machine relied as much on the participation of smaller banks as it did on the funding and syndicating power of the bigger banks.*

This was not surprising: the international banking system had gone through its radical, indiscriminate phase of the early 1970s, had retrenched after Herstatt and Franklin, then had quickly decided that there was no real danger at all and resumed in earnest. The regionals followed the lead of the large banks, as always, especially in the syndicated loans. Most of them operated overseas the same way Cleveland Trust did, dispatching small staffs of calling officers to cover huge regions of the globe. Most had the same basic lending philosophy: international business existed in order to support domestic business, and their goal was to provide trade finance in support of U.S. overseas sales. A big bank such as Chase Manhattan often operated as a local bank wherever it had branches, conducting business that frequently had nothing to do with American trade. Regionals rarely did this: they might have branches overseas, but by and large stayed away from pure international finance.

A loan portfolio of a vice-president in the international division at First Wisconsin, at Wachovia in North Carolina, or at Connecticut Bank

* See appendix.

and Trust would have the same eccentric look that Hammel's portfolio had: both would have short-term lines of credit to a number of foreign banks, few of which would be actively used; both would have the odd loan to a foreign importer of one of their domestic client's products; both would have participations in large syndicates. The game may have been played by the big banks' rules, but the participation of the regionals was critical to the success of the larger system.

2

HAMMEL HAD been able to do something distinctly un-regional in Israel, which was in fact the only country in the world where Cleveland Trust approached the status of a big-time bank. Why Israel? And how could a mere $40 million put the bank in that league? It was a strange choice for a midwestern bank with a management passionately opposed to lending money anywhere there was political and economic turmoil. In 1979, Israel matched that description better than all but a few of the world's principal sovereign borrowers. It was a tiny country surrounded by large, hostile neighbors. It had fought three major wars in the last two decades. Economically, it was much worse off than Algeria. It had very little oil (which it later had to give back to Egypt) and no other major source of hard-currency income. Its foreign debt had risen from $4 billion in 1973 to $15 billion in 1979. Its annual trade deficit was $2.5 billion and rising, and its debt service was running at 30 percent, well above the 20 percent benchmark that international lenders consider prudent. The organizing mechanism of its domestic economy was an insidious policy known as "indexation," which tied salaries, interest rates, and investments to the cost-of-living index. It had removed much of inflation's burden from the average Israeli, who was more than happy to let the government continue to foot the bill by printing money, running larger and larger deficits, and borrowing more and more foreign money. If an Israeli deposited $1,000 at a bank and prices doubled, he would be credited with $2,000 on deposit, and would pay taxes only on the 3 or 4 percent nominal interest, not on principal growth. Indexed salaries were raised by up to 25 percent a month. And as more and more of the economy was indexed, it became impossible to de-index any single part of it. Interest on bank loans exceeded 150 percent per annum. Against all this, the Israeli shekel was rapidly depreciating, making the burden of foreign debt even heavier. To make its problems worse, military spending had risen to a staggering 38 percent of the country's gross national product.

A catalogue that gloomy would normally insure a quick death for any proposed loan in Cleveland Trust's credit committees. But it did not. Of all the Middle Eastern countries, including Kuwait, which had the highest per capita income in the world, Israel was the easiest ride in the loan committees, even though it had no reasonable near-term prospect of earning enough hard currency to repay its loans. The reason for that had much to do with international politics and the political bent of the bank's chairman, and little or nothing to do with traditional bank credit standards. If you relied strictly on numbers, on the behavior of the economy, you had to conclude that Israel was in trouble. Its inflation rate, debt service, foreign trade deficit, and its inability to earn foreign exchange made it a bad credit risk in anybody's book. But viewed politically and emotionally, the situation seemed quite different. Israel was the principal ally of the U.S. in the Middle East, and its security was explicitly guaranteed by our government. More tangibly, the U.S. provided some $1.8 billion in annual aid, $1 billion of which went into the military. The country had access to foreign "political" capital in the form of national bonds, which were held by Jews and Jewish sympathizers around the world, and which made up most of the country's debt. It received half a billion dollars in reparations from Germany each year. The idea was that the U.S., or worldwide Jewry, or some combination of the two, would never let the country fail, either militarily or economically, since the two were closely related.

A look at Israel's economic condition five years later shows how truly political the lending was and continues to be. In 1984, the country's debt had doubled again to $29.3 billion, giving it the second highest per capita foreign debt in the world. The annual trade deficit had deteriorated to $2.66 billion, and the country's debt service was 32.7 percent of exports, still well above the benchmark level. After five years, nothing had changed: All that had happened was that another $14 billion or so had been drained from the economy and replaced by debt. And now the occupation of Lebanon was costing a million dollars a day. The only thing that kept Israel alive was a political commitment by the monied world to maintain its existence. And Cleveland Trust as a major bank lender was its beneficiary.

Israel is an extreme example of the politics of foreign lending. But to varying degrees this sort of thing had been going on for years, and would become more common as the debt of developing countries fell further and further into arrears. The fact was that political considerations had come to replace traditional credit standards as a rationale for bank lending. The shah of Iran was a popular debtor as much for his role as a staunch U.S. ally as for his oil wells. The financial community could comfort itself with the knowledge that the U.S. would never abandon such a valuable friend. In Eastern Europe, most bank lending was based on the so-called "umbrella theory," which had come into vogue after detente. The theory held that loans to Poland, Rumania, Czechoslovakia or other Comecon (Warsaw Pact) countries were ultimately guaranteed by the might of the Soviet Empire, even though no single loan contract carried such a guarantee; it assumed that, in the final analysis, the Soviet Union would not let one of its satellites go down. This was proven to be disastrously wrong in Poland, just as confidence in the shah proved to be misplaced. But politics served as the basic rationale for those loans, as it did with Cleveland Trust in Israel. After the series of sovereign defaults in the early 1980s, politics would come ultimately to be the only rationale for lending, as the U.S. government, the Federal Reserve, and the IMF became the critical players in the game.

If Hammel owed his freedom from restraint in Israel to this, his actions also mirrored the policies of M. Brock Weir, chairman of the board of the Cleveland Trust Company. Upon his arrival from the Bank of California in 1972, one of Weir's first moves was to buy 17 percent of a British bank called Bank Leumi, U.K., a subsidiary of the largest and most powerful bank in Israel, Bank Leumi le-Israel. Soon after, Weir engineered the purchase of $5 million of Israel government bonds. By the time Hammel started to travel regularly to the country, the door had been opened wide. Before the middle of the decade, Hammel had made $20 million in loans to Bank Leumi le-Israel, and another $5 million to its subsidiary, Union Bank of Israel. He had parlayed his connections with the country into loans to equipment dealers, chemical companies, and even the central bank of Israel. He had secured approval for an unprecedented $10-million loan to a federation of kibbutzim, the first time a Western bank had done that. Weir, meanwhile, had had a forest named for him in Israel and continued to support the bank's lending policies to the country. Cleveland Trust had the closest relationship with Israel's largest bank of any major American bank, the only equity partnership in an overseas subsidiary of an Israeli bank. This was odd, since in every other major borrowing country the Citibanks and Chases of the world had long had a lock on that sort of thing. But not in Israel. In fact, since the early 1970s, they had treated the country like a leper colony, and many of them refused even to travel there. It is not hard to guess the reason: Since the first oil crisis, they had been on the receiving end of billions of dollars of OPEC deposits, much of which had come from Saudi Arabia, Kuwait, and the United Arab Emirates, all avowed enemies of the state of Israel. If Saudi Arabia had discovered that Bank of America was lending money to Israel, it would have pulled all of its Eurodeposits out of the bank in a matter of hours, and those deposits were funding much of the Bank of America's foreign loans. So the big banks would trade Israel off in favor of the Arab markets in North Africa and the Middle East. And Cleveland Trust had found itself, by default, as one of Israel's major banks.

Even stranger, though, was the fact that Cleveland Trust had not made the same trade-off in reverse. Hammel continued to travel and solicit Arab borrowers. How could the bank do this? The answer was that our portfolio was so small, relatively, that we could slip in and out among the adversary countries without causing a stir. Every year Hammel did his best to keep any mention of Israel out of the bank's annual report, in spite of the marketing people's desire to put it in. When we traveled in the Middle East, we held two separate passports. To get to Tel Aviv from an Arab country (in the days before the Tel Aviv–Cairo flights), we would travel to Cyprus to "cleanse" our passports. As we passed through outgoing customs in Cyprus, we would change our regular passports with Arab stamps for our clean passports that bore only the stamp of Israel. The point was to keep that Israel immigration stamp out of your normal passport, because customs officials in Kuwait or Damascus would look for it. If they found it, they would almost certainly deny you entrance into the country. With our double passports, Hammel and I were able to bridge the two worlds, to keep them both separate and active. We were successful—a year later, Abu Dhabi would place $200 million of its national pension fund with our trust department, with no apparent knowledge that they were hiring a trustee that actively supported the state of Israel.

As of this writing, Weir's reliance on world politics to shore up his loan portfolio in Israel has been successful. But no country can run huge annual payments deficits forever, nor can it go on supporting its indexation habits with foreign loans indefinitely. Mexico and Brazil proved that even the most favored of borrowers, with the easiest access to money, can go broke overnight if the tap is shut off. How much further can Israel go? Its debt has doubled in the last five years; will it double again? Unless its trade balance changes, it will indeed. At some point there will have to be a reckoning, when even the most charitable and sympathetic of the country's supporters will begin to demand some sort of fiscal responsibility. When that happens, you will see "moratoria," "rescheduling," and the intervention of the IMF, just as in Latin America.

Chapter Seven

TROUBLE IN PARADISE

*On the whole, the greater the earlier reputation for omnis-
cience, the more serene the previous idiocy, the greater the
foolishness now exposed. Things that in other times were
concealed behind a heavy facade of dignity now stood exposed, for the panic suddenly, almost obscenely, snatched
this facade away.*

—J. K. GALBRAITH,
The Great Crash of 1929

1

IN THE spring of 1981, things were looking very good for Ben Bailey,
senior vice-president and head of Cleveland Trust's international division. In the past decade he had risen from an obscure position as a trust
officer to lead one of the bank's major lending divisions. From his large
corner office on the ninth floor, he oversaw an expanding financial empire that already dwarfed most commercial banks in the United States:
at his immediate disposal were more than $800 million in assets, sev-
enteen marketing officers, forty operations personnel, and a foreign exchange department.

In 1976, his career had taken one of those amazing jumps that happened so often during the boom years of international banking. Bailey

knew international trade, having traveled the world as a salesman for an automotive company. But he had little experience in international finance. In fact, he had never before been employed as an international banker. And he had been promoted from the trust department, which had little or nothing to do with anything foreign, and nothing at all to do with lending. He was lucky: His promotion happened to coincide with the beginning of the second great cycle of foreign lending in the 1970s, in which regional banks, for the first time, became large-scale participants.

Under Bailey's guidance, the division had nearly doubled in size, and the bank's foreign loan portfolio had undergone a prodigious expansion. Bailey was making the bank a lot of money. With only sixty or so of the bank's thirty-five hundred employees, he earned 10 percent of Cleveland Trust's bottom-line profits. That spring he could boast almost a decade of lending with few problem loans and fewer write-offs, a record none of the bank's other corporate lending divisions could match. Bailey was an optimist by nature, and by 1981 he had good reason to be optimistic about his future.

What Bailey did not see were the thunderheads on the horizon. By December 31, 1982, more than $200 million in loans would be in trouble in Mexico, Brazil, Venezuela, Poland, and the Philippines. The events of the next two years would shake the division to its foundations, and would set in motion a series of purges, departures, and restructurings that would leave it almost unrecognizable. By 1984, thirteen of the seventeen officers who had staffed the division in 1980 would be gone, and Ben Bailey, his deputy manager, and most of the members of the senior credit committee that approved the foreign loans would take early retirements. The severe backlash from the domestic bank would cause the division's portfolio to contract by more than $130 million by the end of 1984. The same thing would happen, to greater and lesser degrees, at every international bank in the United States.

Poland was the harbinger of disaster. In March 1981, Poland's chief borrowing officer told seventy representatives of more than five hundred banks—Cleveland Trust among them—that Poland was broke. The banks had believed in the umbrella theory, which assumed that the Soviet Union would not allow one of its satellites to default on its foreign loans. But now the theory was shattered, and it was too late to do anything about it. The loans would be assigned to the twilight zone of rescheduled sovereign debt, where they would sit pending what the banks hoped would be the eventual solvency of the Polish government. Officially, Cleveland Trust's loans were not bad loans—because if they were, then some $25 billion in loans to the Polish government were also bad and would have to be written off. At the very least, that would destroy West Germany's biggest banks, which had a disproportionate share of the debt, and would cause panic in the U.S. money markets, and no one wanted that. It was Cleveland Trust's first lesson in the safety of numbers—toward which its management would have an increasingly ambivalent attitude. But for Ben Bailey and his staff of lending officers, the bloom was already off the rose.

Conditions in the debt markets would get rapidly worse. In September 1981, eleven months before the Mexican crisis destroyed the last of the comforting illusions harbored by Cleveland Trust's senior management, a $10-million loan to a Philippine construction company—the bank's first and only term loan in that country—would fall in arrears on its payments. Payments would falter for the next several years. After being taken over by the government in 1983, the company ran out of money altogether.

Although Cleveland Trust was finally able to recoup all but some $700,000 of its loan—before the Philippines stopped paying its debt—along the way it had one of the roughest rides in the international debt market, one that showed plainly the risks that a regional bank ran in an opaque, alien economy 12,000 miles away. The story of the loan shows how a regional bank found itself in trouble and well out of its depth abroad, a story that would be mirrored on a much larger scale in the experiences of other regional banks in the Third World in the years after 1982.

I had been intimately involved in that loan as a calling officer in the bank's Asia/Pacific area. As a participant in the frail logical system that justified it, I understood for the first time in my career what it meant to be dead wrong about a foreign client.

2

WHEN I landed in Manila in the spring of 1980, after a twenty-one-day Cook's tour of the Orient, a bad loan was the last thing on my mind. Bad loans were, for the most part, not part of the repertoire of the international loan officer, as the clever moratoria, reschedulings, and other euphemistic two-stepping in Indonesia, Zaire, Peru, Chile, and Turkey had demonstrated. In a world where no sovereign could go bankrupt, and no bank would ever call or write off a sovereign loan, there was a certain built-in safety. As an international money salesman, I thought only of making the loans, of bumping up my loan portfolio, of being rewarded with a raise, and not of what I was going to do if my loans went bad. It was not, after all, in my power to *approve* those loans anyway (I had personal approval limit of $100,000, carefully calculated to be almost completely worthless in international banking). I merely presented the menu from which the senior credit committee selected. The bank had never lost a cent in Asia, to my knowledge. I had never seen a bad foreign loan at close hand, nor had I been trained in how to recover one. I had come into Manila on an omen-ridden flight from Taipei. The problems had started 31,000 feet over the South China Sea, when the 707 had taken an abrupt 5,000-foot dive toward the blue water below, sending flight attendants and the contents of the duty-free sales carts careening about the aircraft. No explanation came from the cockpit or from the attendants. Across from me in the first-class compartment, the Maharishi Mahesh Yogi buckled his seatbelt. An hour later, the plane hit a severe thunderstorm over the mountains of Luzon which seemed as though it were about to shatter the 20-year-old airframe, and was even more frightening than our dive over the South China Sea.

In Manila the sky was freshening after the rain. My fear of death had quickly gone, aided by the generous portions of free liquor you get in first class, and it felt good to be a banker again. I was twenty-six years old, and I had traveled to twenty-six countries in the last eight months. I liked the travel, staying in nice hotels, the intellectual exercise of trying to figure out what sort of deals were going down in the financial subworlds of Hong Kong, Tel Aviv, and Kuala Lumpur. I enjoyed thinking of how it would feel to be a Citibank syndicator, lunching with the head of the central bank and launching billion-dollar project loans. Then I was met at the airport by a shiny new Mercedes, which also contained a girl. She told me that she and the car were at my disposal during my stay in the Philippines. And there was a plane waiting to take me to Baguio, a fabulous mountain resort in the north, near the country of the rice terraces where her employers owned a hotel. A weekend on them, if I wanted.

Why was this youthful representative of a small U.S. bank being treated this way? Because Cleveland Trust had approved $10 million of credit for the company that owned the girl, the Mercedes, and the hotel in Baguio to buy earthmoving equipment from the U.S. Just prior to my trip to Asia, the company had begun to borrow on this credit, taking off million-dollar chunks to pay for shipments of material and equipment.

For Cleveland Trust, this loan had been a stroke of unimaginable good luck, a rare Asian lending coup. The Philippines, both private and public sectors, was among the world's most active borrowers. The country's credit rating was excellent, and the big banks had been muscling in on the prime business for years. Against competition from some of the most voracious international banks in the world, we had swung a deal with one of the country's largest companies, and we had done it the way the bank wanted it, in support of clients' trade. Sitting at lunch overlooking the Pagsanhan River, flanked by the Mercedes and the girl, sipping a tall gin drink, and relishing the brief feeling of self-importance, it all seemed too good to be true.

And in fact it was. While we were congratulating ourselves on Cleveland Trust's stunning incursion into the territories of the big banks, our client was already in trouble. Before it had borrowed the entire $10 million it would be in serious trouble. Two years later it would be on the brink of bankruptcy. What I was really experiencing there at Pagsanhan was the gratitude of a desperate creditor who had found a bank willing to lend it money when almost no one else would. I did not know this then; no one in the international division suspected it. We knew that we had made a loan to one of the largest construction companies in Asia, and that it was guaranteed by the soundest blue-chip creditor in the Philippines. Even if the company went under, we were still supported by the full faith and credit of the Philippine government. We did not know that the bank would later be forced to play this trump card, as the Philippines ran out of all foreign exchange to pay off its debt.

How had we come to make that loan? It had all begun innocently enough in the early 1970s. In that decade, trade in the Pacific basin had begun to bloom. The economies of Korea, Japan, Hong Kong, Taiwan, Singapore, the Philippines, and Malaysia were sustaining phenomenal growth rates, the highest in the world. U.S. multinationals were investing heavily in the area, and with the economic boom came a brisk two-way trade with the U.S.

As the U.S. corporations moved west across the Pacific, so, faithfully, did Cleveland Trust. In 1972 Cleveland Trust hired M. Brock

Weir, former chairman of Bank of California, as it chairman. Bank of California was a medium-sized bank, but had an unusually active international division, so Weir was accustomed to the slicker, more sophisticated international trade. He brought with him a young man named Michael Clemens, who had run Bank of California's representative office in Manila, and appointed him head of the international division. Clemens knew the Philippines and had many contacts. He made the first trips there for Cleveland Trust beginning in 1973.

In 1974, Rick Herrick, in his mid-twenties and a few years out of a credit-training program at a Pittsburgh bank, became the bank's chief calling officer in Asia and began traveling regularly to the Philippines. The Philippine strategy, as concocted by Clemens and Herrick, was to call heavily on Philippine banks, try to hustle lines of credit (short-term borrowings that the banks would use to fund their trade portfolios), and hunt down both U.S. multinationals and the local companies who bought U.S. goods and services. But while banks' credits were regarded as both safe and profitable (which meant that you could sell them to the loan committees), what Clemens and Herrick were really after were loans that funded Philippine purchases of U.S. goods. The trick was to discover the trade connections, to ferret out who was selling to whom. This strategy would not change substantially until the fall of 1981.

From the beginning, Clemens and Herrick had found the going very rough, the competition unusually fierce. Since Marcos had imposed martial law in 1972, the Philippines had been an immensely popular creditor. The Americans had begun to crowd in during the mid-1970s, opening offices that ranged from full branches, to "offshore banking units," to rep offices of the sort that Mike Clemens had run for Weir at the Bank of California. There were good economic reasons to be there: the country was growing at 6.5 percent a year through the decade and was borrowing heavily on foreign markets. And, it was impossible to deny, the Philippines was one of the most pleasant places on earth to do business. The people were generous and hospitable. With martial law, the security problems of the late 1960s had vanished. American expatriates lived in large, airy bungalows around Makati, Manila's sparkling new glass-and-steel business district. They usually had several servants, and they often had their own drivers to negotiate the hellish traffic jams for which Makati was famous. For the single male, or for the prodigal married man, Manila was the R&R capital of Asia. There were some of the best golf courses in the world around Manila. The financial world in Manila was so small—the equivalent of about half a block on Wall Street—that everyone knew everyone else; they had parties, played golf, went to hostess bars together, and of course passed each other business. Filipino business is a high-spirited, high-speed social game, and true, unaffected friendliness is as important as business skill.

But Cleveland Trust had chosen not to open an office in the Philippines, and so had shut itself off from the clubby world of local finance in which other American and foreign banks were so deeply and comfortably ensconced. Clemens and Herrick were thus reduced to the old hunt-and-peck method of foreign solicitation. Spending less than two weeks a year in the country precluded almost all inside knowledge, and inside knowledge was what led you to new business in the Philippines. While the banks with local offices did a brisk business, Cleveland Trust found nothing.

As the years went by, the going got even rougher. In 1977, Alec Bigelson, a sartorial, bearded thirty-year-old with a law degree, took over the Asia Pacific area from Herrick, who had moved to take charge of the bank's portfolio in Latin America. In 1977, Bigelson hired a twenty-four-year-old named Tim Reynolds, and together they kept up the canvassing efforts in the Philippines. I joined the area (splitting my time with Hammel in the Middle East) in 1978. But after some six years of calling in the Philippines, of tracking every trade connection that could be dug up, and after tens of thousands of dollars had been spent on travel, all the Asia Pacific area of the international division had to show for its trouble was a $2-million line of credit to the cash-starved Philippine National Oil Company—hardly a prestigious deal since the company had several hundred creditor banks, almost all of whom had larger lines of credit than Cleveland Trust—and a couple of paltry lines of credit to Philippine banks, which went unused.

Meanwhile, Ben Bailey had replaced Clemens as head of the division. From the first it had bothered the salesman in him that in both Taiwan and the Philippines, where other banks were finding business and making millions from loans and deposits, Cleveland Trust was being frozen out. Bailey wanted "term exposure"—five- or seven-year loans that would guarantee a steady flow of interest income to the bottom line. The problem—as Bailey's officers did not fail to perceive—was that just *any* term loan would not do. Herrick and Bigelson had had plenty of chances to participate in those gargantuan "balance of payments" loans to the Philippine government, from which much of Citicorp's and Bank of America's profits were coming. Brock Weir did not approve of indiscriminate sovereign lending, and his senior credit committee was a faithful reflection of his preferences. The loan would have to be to a top-notch Philippine company; it would have to fund the purchase of goods from a domestic client. Then, after six years of looking for that combination, Bailey's luck suddenly turned. A company called the Construction and Development Company of the Philippines (CDCP) a user of large quantities of heavy U.S. construction equipment, wanted money, and lots of it. What they wanted, specifically, was to buy earth-moving equipment from a company called Terex, a subsidiary of General Motors headquartered in a little town south of Cleveland.

The business was unexpected. We had solicited the company, which, like most other companies in the Philippines, had been gracious and hospitable. It was one of the fastest-growing companies in the Philippines. Its president, Rodolfo "Rudy" Cuenca, was a close friend of President Marcos. The company had begun modestly enough in 1966 as the Cuenca Construction Company. But in the 1970s Cuenca's Marcos connection began to pay off in the form of government-financed infrastructure projects, the largest of which was the $1-billion, 2,700-hectare Manila Bay Reclamation project. CDCP was soon the largest construction company in Southeast Asia, with construction crews scattered all over the Middle East and the Orient. And now this huge, reputable company was asking us for $10 million to buy equipment from Terex. It looked like a perfect deal.

There was only one problem: in order to fund its growth, the company had taken on a huge amount of debt, so much that its debt-to-equity ratio had risen to more than 4 to 1. The banker's rule of thumb—in those years, anyway—was that 1 to 1 leverage is healthy, 2 to 1 suspect, and 3 to 1 unsupportable. CDCP, the golden opportunity after six years of fruitless calling, would never make it past the credit committees. But there was a way to solve the problem, using the same panacea that many international banks had been relying on for years: get the sovereign government to guarantee it. Never mind that the Philippines had already borrowed too much money, or that it had put its name on far more guarantees than it could reasonably pay off. Those were highly subjective considerations, impossible to prove. So Cuenca would be leaned on to persuade Marcos to order the Philippine National Bank to issue a "standby letter of credit," a form of conditional guarantee of payment of principal and interest at a rate of 6 percent per annum. The promise of the full faith and credit of the Philippines was enough to sway the senior loan committees, and they approved $10 million worth of credit to finance the exports of Terex and any other U.S. company who was an existing or target customer. It was the kind of deal that Weir was thought to favor: an ironclad, guaranteed credit to finance customer trade.

3

WHILE I was happily sipping my gin by the Pagsanhan River in 1980, CDCP had begun to draw down quickly on its credit. Shipments of earth-moving equipment from Terex were arriving monthly, and with each one, I would examine the documentation, verify shipment, and disburse a million or two dollars. The money went directly to Terex and was immediately recorded on our books as a five-year loan to CDCP. And so CDCP was going out of its way to make me comfortable. They took me to dinner at La Tasca, one of the most expensive restaurants in the city. They took me to play golf. They reminded me that a plane was fueled and ready to take off for Baguio if I wanted. The Mercedes waited patiently at my hotel.

But as I accepted their splendid hospitality, my calls elsewhere in Manila produced some unsettling news. I began hearing the rumors that the local business community had been hearing for a long time, and that the Asian press would trumpet across the Orient two years later. "CDCP is growing very fast," one local banker told me over lunch, "but maybe too fast. I don't know where they are going to find the money or the management to keep that up." At the big trading companies, I was told that CDCP was the slowest "pay" in the country. One of them said: "They're not slow pay, they don't pay at all. Everybody knows it." At another call, I was told by one of CDCP's suppliers that his company would no longer do business with them unless they paid their back invoices. What they were suggesting was that our prime client was in the middle of a cash-flow crisis of huge proportions. A big company like that usually sets the terms with smaller companies. Now the roles were being reversed, and the smaller companies were beginning to dictate their own terms. I had started my Manila calls by proclaiming proudly that we were one of CDCP's major banks; after years of humbly admitting that we had little or no exposure in the country, it was good to trot out a prime borrower to hype our "lending capabilities." I had managed to draw only a slightly bewildered silence, as though I had said something embarrassing. At Philippine National Bank, I was not met by our usual contact but by a junior assistant who smiled, looked vaguely ill at ease, and did not seem terribly eager to talk about their standby letter of credit or about CDCP. By the end of my visit, I had decided not to mention the loan to anyone. Something was clearly wrong.

Back in Cleveland, the company was borrowing at a furious rate. By the end of the year it would have its full ten million, and there was no way to stop it. I discussed what I had heard with my boss, Alec Bigelson. We reviewed the company's last financial statement and saw no appreciable change. Whatever the company's problems, from 12,000 miles away they were quite invisible. We took comfort in the PNB guarantee and told ourselves that there was nothing we could really do except watch it, if worst came to worst, we would simply "draw" under the terms of the standby letter of credit. As long as the economy of the Philippines was intact, we would get our money back. We had no idea then how precarious that guarantee would be.

In September 1981, the rumors turned into fact. CDCP missed a large principal payment. It was characteristic of the international banking business that by then none of the officers who had worked on the original loan were still working at the bank. Tim Reynolds had left in 1980, I had left in 1981 to take a job with United California Bank, and Alec Bigelson had taken a job running Security Pacific Bank's Cleveland Office. Our successors, Rick Smith, who had come from First National Bank of Maryland, and a twenty-five-year-old named Jeff Jones with several years in the division's export finance department, quickly found themselves confronted with a loan they had not been responsible for and did not fully understand to a company in serious trouble. We who had made the loan would not be there to clean it up.

The September payment deadline came and went with no word from the company. CDCP did not return telex requests for money. Several weeks passed. Jeff Jones began calling overseas from his home late at night, and he finally got through. He was told that the money was coming, that he should go to bed and not worry. Infuriated, yet unable to do anything about it from 12,000 miles away, he returned to work the next day to report CDCP's promise—and to begin to figure out what the hell was going on in the Philippines.

Feeling helpless and uninformed, Smith and Jones had only two immediate options: to seek the advice of in-house legal counsel; or to try to find out who CDCP's other creditors were, and to see if those banks knew any more than they did.

What they found was curious indeed. Most of CDCP's foreign creditors in the past few years had not been the big money center banks at all, nor were they even banks who had in-country offices. Instead, they were a motley collection of smaller regionals, and all had the same reason for lending to CDCP: to fund clients' exports. The implication was uncomfortably obvious—our brilliant coup had not been the result of hard work, persistence, or even pure luck. We had not made this loan by beating the big international banks to the punch. It was not an accident that CDCP had gone hunting for money among regional banks with no local offices, and therefore no access to the local grapevine. Our loan had been among its last, desperate attempts to raise foreign capital and save itself from extinction. CDCP had, in effect, taken advantage of the very conservatism that had kept all those regional banks out of big-time foreign lending. Later in my career, when I was working on the Philippines desk at First Interstate Bank of California, I asked the bank's former Philippine branch manager about CDCP. She told me that she had had several opportunities to lend them money, but had deliberately stayed away. The company had "problems," she said, and everyone there more or less knew it.

Not so at Cleveland Trust. Events in the Philippines were moving much too fast. In 1981, CDCP's income plummeted from $13 million to $2 million. The company was vastly overextended and deeply in debt. Unable to secure loans from the foreign banks, it managed to get a $35-million credit from the Central Bank of the Philippines. But this was not enough to save it. In desperation, Cuenca played the Marcos card again and got the Development Bank of the Philippines and the Philippine National Bank to purchase 30 percent of its equity, a net capital injection of $110 million. And still it was bleeding cash so fast that it missed principal payments with Cleveland Trust and the other regionals.

One of the main reasons for its troubles was that Cuenca had been foolish enough to accept land rather than cash in payment for much of the work on the reclamation project. Smith and Jones learned this from Republic National Bank of Dallas. The banks with local offices had known about it all along. We had never heard it before, and it had been one of our assumptions that the reclamation project would help pay off our loan.

Unable to do anything about CDCP, Smith and Jones turned to Lew Perelman, the in-house legal counsel, for advice on the PNB standby letter of credit. Could they accelerate maturity and draw against it? They hauled the document out of the files and headed up to the legal department. Perelman told them that there were problems; Cleveland Trust might not be able to draw. He drafted amendments to the letter of credit— ones that would guarantee a payout if CDCP defaulted—and dispatched them to Manila in November to try to straighten things out with PNB and set up a meeting with the principals at CDCP. A few weeks before their trip to Manila, the loan payment came in, some forty-five days late.

In the Philippines, Smith and Jones found PNB cooperative and helpful. At CDCP they were assured that there would be no further problems. The CDCP managers took them to an expensive dinner; they suggested a night on the town, which Smith and Jones declined. Both came away with the feeling that CDCP was not to be trusted—and that from then on, they would consider the PNB guarantee the sole security on the loan. They delivered Perelman's signed agreements. The credit was rock-solid now, unless the Philippines itself went broke.

During the next two years, both CDCP and the Republic of the Philippines proceeded to run rapidly out of foreign capital. It was only a question of who would go broke first, or whether they would fall together. In the Middle East, CDCP was reeling from the dual effects of its aggressive underbidding and increased foreign competition. In the Philippines, it was suffering from slow payment by government agencies. In February, the government canceled $133 million in debt in exchange for 500 hectares of land in the reclamation project. In May 1982, the *Far Eastern Economic Review* reported that CDCP needed $250 million immediately to pay off debt, and that the company was in the midst of a serious crisis. In January 1983, the central bank loaned it another $35 million. On February 23, 1983, President Marcos signed a presidential directive ordering the government takeover of CDCP, a final gesture of cronyism which Jaime Ongpin, a leading Filipino businessman, called "The most obscene, brazen, and disgraceful misallocation of taxpayers' money in the history of the Philippines."

During this time, payments to Cleveland Trust faltered, stopped, then began intermittently again until it was clear in the summer of 1983 that, even though it had been nationalized, the company as an operating unit was nearly extinct. The effect of the government takeover of CDCP meant that, for all practical purposes, the bank's guarantee from the government-owned Philippine National Bank was now moot. Cleveland Trust's "private sector" loan had suddenly turned into a pure government loan. The problem now was that the Philippines itself was about to become insolvent. Although the government managed to make good on much of the remaining debt during 1983, some $700,000 ended up unrepaid—frozen when the country suspended all principal payments on foreign debt in October 1983.

By the time that happened, the revolving door had spun again on the ninth floor. Rick Smith had left the division for a domestic assignment and Jeff Jones had taken a job with an investment bank. A young officer named Auctstolis had taken charge of the Asia/Pacific area. Bailey was still there—but now as a lame duck, presiding over an empire that was in deep trouble and shrinking fast. A few months later Charles Hammel would replace him as head of the division.

4

MORE THAN four hundred U.S. banks were swept up in the Philippines debt catastrophe. It was the final payoff of their unwillingness to control the country's borrowing habits. When the CDCP loan was first approved, the total external debt of the Philippines stood at some $12 billion. In the forecasts and country studies, this looked like a manageable number. The economy was still growing at 6 percent a year, and its prospects for making foreign exchange off its exports looked favorable. There seemed to be plenty of foreign exchange around to enable the company to repay, in dollars, a five-year, $10-million loan. The implicit, horribly wrong assumption was that the Philippines would not go wild on the foreign debt markets in the next few years and borrow itself into a credit crisis. Yet this is exactly what it did after the second oil price increase. It was the same old story, familiar from the string of sovereign defaults in Latin America. Rather than impose a politically unpopular domestic austerity program, the country's economists, bankers, and politicians simply took on more debt in order to hold the status quo. By 1984 it would be in hock for $25.6 billion to 483 creditor banks and a host of foreign governments. Neither Cleveland Trust nor the big banks had any control of how much the country borrowed. This violates the universal rule of banking procedure involving term loans: You must always be able to control the borrower's indebtedness. We could, and did, make CDCP sign covenants to that effect, but we could never enforce discipline on the government of the Philippines. Any bank that tried to would have been laughed at, or shunned. The market was just too competitive.

The Philippines is one place where the banks should have had control. Yet, there were several built-in dangers. The country relied heavily on oil imports and was equally dependent on its traditional exports: coconut products, sugarcane, minerals (copper, chromite), textiles, and assorted agricultural products such as hemp, coffee, tobacco, and lumber. A rise in the price of the former or a fall in the latter would be disastrous; yet that is what happened between 1979 and 1982. To finance the huge deficit this shortfall produced, the country began to borrow more and more money, even though realistically it did not have the export base to pay that money back. In 1982, the country's debt shot past $20 billion, and the borrowings were at ever shorter maturities, reflecting the banks' growing concerns. But by shortening the maturities of the new loans, the banks were creating a dangerous "bunching" of maturities in the near term, and thereby cutting their own throats. In early 1983, of the $21 billion in total debt, 44 percent, or $9.1 billion, was due. By October, predictably, the country had run out of money and appealed to the banks and the IMF for a ninety-day "moratorium," which would be rolled over into a series of 90-day moratoria.

The effect on the economy, which was accustomed to a constant flow of imports, was staggering. When the Philippines suspended principal payments on its debt in October 1983, it also slapped heavy restrictions on the use of foreign exchange by Philippine corporations and Philippine nationals. Foreign exchange was now rationed to pay only for oil imports, fertilizer, and other agricultural products needed to feed the nation. As the crisis worsened, many of the now-familiar hallmarks of a sovereign debt crisis began to appear: a severe capital flight from the Philippines, further depleting its small foreign exchange reserves; a progressive devaluation of the peso, forced by the banks and by the IMF; and an 80-percent rise in the cost of living for the average Filipino by mid-1984. In the middle of this, it was discovered that the Philippine Central Bank had deliberately inflated its foreign exchange reserves by $1.8 billion.

By this time, the story sounded depressingly familiar.

5

IT IS difficult to find the moral in this tale. We had been wrong about the financial health of CDCP. One might argue that we should never have been out there in the first place, soliciting loans in a patently dangerous economy we did not understand, where American banks had far less legal control than they do in the United States. But that simply ignores the reality of world trade. Try explaining to the line workers at Terex (or Ford, or Boeing, or Caterpillar, all of which employ tens of thousands of Americans and have substantial overseas sales) that they were being laid off because no one was willing to finance the company's foreign trade.

Trade must go on, and to have trade you must have finance. The question is where to draw the line. Here the logic becomes abstruse. Perhaps since Cleveland Trust had no offices in the Philippines it had no business making loans there. But an office—whether for a one-man representative or a twenty-man offshore banking unit—presupposes overhead costs, and in the cost-and-profit-conscious banking world, that almost always means a certain minimum portfolio. Had Bigelson, Reynolds, and I been stationed in the Philippines, we would probably have known better than to make that loan. But we would have made others, and probably many of them. Bank of California, for which Clemens had been the Philippines rep in the early 1970s, had $70 million in loans in the Philippines frozen solid in the moratorium as of December 31, 1983. The same thing might have happened to Cleveland Trust. Under the circumstances, we fared better.

Still the crisis itself could probably have been avoided had the IMF been enlisted earlier, and in a better cause. Sovereigns, like private-sector borrowers, should have had strict, IMF-monitored limits on their ability to take on new debt—limits that would have protected the banks from their own aggressive instincts. Such a debt formula would have to be complex—involving debt service ratios, average loan life and maturity analysis, and continuous monitoring of a country's foreign exchange and short-term debt positions—but it would be no more complex than the current austerity programs and reschedulings. It would be built into all foreign loans, both public and private, since from the perspective of sovereign risk the two are ultimately the same. Once a country hit its upper limit, it would trigger what amounted to default clauses and be forced to retrench, to adopt austerity measures such as currency deval-

uation and foreign exchange controls. Such a formula would have un-
doubtedly led to a series of minidefaults and minicrises. But the scale
would have been much smaller and more manageable. The horrific re-
sults of unregulated bank lending could have been avoided. Also, such
adjustments are nothing new. The Philippines, for example, has signed
seventeen adjustment agreements with the IMF over the past twenty
years. It was only after it had been permitted to go on an unpoliced,
ten-year borrowing spree that the adjustments failed.

Lending in the Philippines was thus never anything but a crap shoot.
Either you got lucky, as Cleveland Trust did, and had only $700,000
frozen in the moratorium, or you did not, like Citibank and hundreds of
others. If there is any lesson to be learned here at all, it is that, in
matters of credit, "empirical" analysis should never be taken as a
wholesale substitute for good common sense. The Philippine experience
proved that bankers could rationalize anything.

Chapter Eight

THE $195-MILLION BURN

1

BROCK WEIR had been looking forward to a smooth, peaceful retirement in 1983, but in August 1982, $116 million of his bank's loans were swept up in an $80-billion sovereign default that went by the ominously neutral name of a "ninety-day moratorium." And there was no clear way out. This amount of troubled debt was enough to cause his board of directors, management, and depositors terrible anxiety; but compared to other banks' exposures it was far too small to give him a meaningful vote in deciding how to get his money back. Senior membership in the new syndicate of bad debt was reserved for those banks that had been *really* wrong about Mexico and had pumped in huge percentages of their capital in loans. Weir's "dues to the club," as he once called his international lending activities, had suddenly made him a nonvoting, junior member in the syndicate. But that was just the beginning.

As with his Polish loans, he had only two choices in Mexico: to swallow his honor and be a good sport while the IMF and the money center banks rewrote the rules; or to declare "events of default," accelerate maturities, and thereby touch off every cross-default clause in every sovereign loan agreement to Mexico, thus bringing down upon himself the disapproval of the world banking community. Cleveland Trust could not single-handedly destroy the agreements upon which Mexico's debt had been postponed, but it could make trouble, not only with its own actions but in influencing those of other regional banks. And therein lay the most bizarre irony of its position. A simultaneous acceleration of maturity and refusal to fund any new loans by many regionals might actually destroy most of America's largest banks. Regionals and smaller banks held 40 percent of all American bank debt in the area, and the money center banks could never absorb that much more. The careful illusion the big banks had created—and sustain to this day—could have been shattered in a few days by uncooperative regionals who believed that by calling in their Latin loans they were protecting their depositors and shareholders. On the other hand, if they cooperated, they would be treated the way they had always been treated in the corridors of international finance—as slightly dull-witted providers of funding, who did not know quite what they were doing and could not be allowed into the "steering committee" rooms where the big decisions were made.

But $116 million was still a lot of money. It was more than 20 percent of the bank's capital and represented 25 percent of all Latin debt held by Ohio banks. Mexico was by far the bank's largest long-term foreign debtor, and second only to Japan in short-term debt. Worse still, 47 percent of the bank's loans had been made, by policy, to the private sector, on the grounds that private-sector lending to support U.S. companies and their exports was safe and prudent, and sovereign balance-of-payments lending was reckless and dangerous. By the end of August 1982, though, it became clear that the private sector was *last in line* for the payouts.

But most nightmarish was the lack of any reasonable recourse. A hundred and sixteen million dollars of midwestern money was caught in an offshore debt storm that no amount of traditional heartland banking technique could help. Ben Bailey—still head of the division but bereft of his old authority—now grimly dispatched loan officers to meetings in New York, where they would sit quietly in the back row, accept the given wisdom, and report back to Cleveland what Citicorp, the Treasury Department, Mexican President López Portillo, and the IMF had decided to do. He had led an $800-million charge into the heart of the international debt market; now he would lead an uncomfortable retreat, presiding quietly over a quickly shrinking portfolio.

Mexico had been the death of the idea, long popular at Cleveland Trust, that you could safely play the edges of the market, nip in with a good supplier credit here or factory loan there, do some short-term lending to the banks and come out of it unscathed. Poland and the Phlippines were unpleasant experiences, but they did not threaten the bank itself. Mexico placed *a fifth* of the bank's capital in direct, unambiguous jeopardy.

The situation in Mexico would deteriorate as the autumn progressed and the depth of the problem became clear. The word that came down in August was that the country was temporarily broke; it had asked for and received a ninety-day moratorium on repayment of principal. But then in September, Jesus Silva Herzog delivered a shocking piece of news: He admitted to a journalist that Mexico was not in a position to pay back any principal until 1984. That month, President López Portillo nationalized the banks, confirming the point that had apparently been lost on Cleveland Trust's management: that private and public debt all came down to the same thing in a foreign exchange crisis.

But if it was too late to do anything about Mexico but watch, Cleveland Trust still had options on the Latin American continent, where it had some $100 million in outstanding debt in Brazil and Venezuela and much more in commitments. It could do nothing about its term loans, but many of its commitments were in the form of "lines of credit"—unilateral commitments to finance borrowers for periods of less than a year. Those lines could be quickly pulled.

In October, that is exactly what Weir decided to do. That month a talented, bilingual thirty-two-year-old named Pedro Mitro, who had taken over from Herrick as head of the Latin American division a few months before, was sent to Brazil and Venezuela to pull in every line of credit he could. Not surprisingly, this same thought had occurred to most of the other 180-odd regional banks as well as to many of the European and Japanese banks which, like Cleveland Trust, had limited exposure, nothing like the stakes of the big New York and London banks. They were unorganized and self-interested—but their collective power was awesome. By simultaneously cutting and running they precipitated an instant, lethal debt crisis in almost every country in Latin America. Brazil, Argentina, Bolivia, Chile, Peru, and Uruguay all defaulted within months of Mexico, and Venezuela would follow in February 1983. The result of Mitro's trip, and the trips of hundreds like him, was a full-scale $300-billion crisis. The banks had thus precipitated the crisis themselves. They did not do it knowingly; like Cleveland Trust, they

all thought they were being smart and prudent. They did not know the
extent of the abandonment of Latin America by their peers; they especially had no idea that countries like Brazil and Venezuela were actually
living off the short-term debt that they were now canceling.

When the size of Brazil's short-term debt was revealed in December,
it rocked the banking world. There is little doubt that the crisis would
eventually have come: the debt service ratios of the countries involved
were too high to avoid it for long. But the sudden, catastrophic default
of the entire continent was no accident. And the regionals, which had
been considered insignificant by the big banks throughout the 1970s and
early 1980s, suddenly found themselves not only prodigiously powerful
as a group, but also, individually, critical to the big banks' survival.
With nearly half of the American loans to Latin America, and with
relatively little to lose by writing them off, they held the fate of Citicorp, Chase, Bank of America, Morgan, Manufacturers Hanover, and
Chemical in their hands.

Mitro's trip south was an unpleasant one. Since 1979 he had been the
division's most productive loan officer, having been responsible for the
majority of the $150 million in loans in Venezuela and Mexico that
were outstanding at the time of the Mexican crisis. His portfolio included subsidiaries of some of the most successful U.S. companies—
names like Eaton, Sears, Harris, and John Deere—all of which he had
courted diligently, both at home and abroad. Now he had to go back
and tell them—without actually saying so—that he was cutting off their
credit. The technique was to tell the client that Cleveland Trust had not
"processed" (i.e., renewed) the company's line of credit because of a
"delay." Nothing was said about the bank's ardent desire to flee Latin
America and never return. Mitro would then ask the company to accept
the formality and pay off whatever outstanding loans it had. Of course
once cleared, the line would be cut, and the company would not be able
to borrow again. There was nothing terribly mysterious about this. The
companies were even getting used to it, and most of them understood
why.

The trip was a success, and a number of companies paid off. But the
aggregate effect of Mitro's and others' actions on the economies of Brazil and Venezuela was devastating. Cleveland Trust's lines of credit
represented immediately available dollars to their cash-starved economies. What was more, they could be rolled over like so much other for-

eign debt, creating the net effect of a long-term dollar credit. Mitro had also cut their bank lines, another important source of dollars to pay for imports of food, oil, raw materials, and industrial products.

The big banks with the largest exposures had done nothing like this. When Brazil had protested in the early autumn that, unlike the rest of Latin America, it had not squandered its borrowings, the big banks believed it and renewed its credits. Venezuela had "revalued" its reserves in September to show how unlike Mexico it, too, was, and the big banks also maintained its lines of credit. But of course the banks desperately wanted to believe it, and ultimately they had no real choice anyway. Bank of America, for example, with $2.5 billion out to Brazil, could not afford to endanger its own portfolio by denying the country short-term credit. But the collective effect of the regionals' actions was very nearly the same as if most of the big U.S. banks had bailed out. By December 1, Brazil, the largest debtor in the Third World, was broke; by February, Venezuela could sustain its illusion of solvency no longer. And so by early 1983, Cleveland Trust was adding another $78 million to its lengthening list of problem loans.

2

NEVER WAS the ignorance of the commercial banks quite as shockingly apparent as it was in Latin America. Mitro's panicky descent in October was not prompted by hard numbers, or certain knowledge of the impending financial collapse of Brazil and Venezuela. Cleveland Trust did not know the size or state of Brazil's foreign-currency reserves, nor did it have the remotest idea—none of the banks did—of the titanic proportions of its short-term debt. Its panic was more the product of an irrational—but, as it turned out, correct—fear, conditioned by the events of the previous six months: the war in the Falklands; the failure of a subsidiary of Banco Ambrosiano, Italy's largest bank, which had touched off a chain of cross-default clauses in Luxembourg; the Penn Square Bank and the Drysdale Securities scandals had broken into the news in late spring and early summer; and rumors of serious trouble at both Continental Illinois and Seattle First National Bank were beginning to spread through the financial markets. All of this made for the sort of jittery financial mood that tends to precede panics. Then, as if to confirm everyone's irrational fear, Mexico had in August introduced the hitherto unimaginable idea that a large industrial country with $80 billion or more in debt could become insolvent in a matter of months. Had it not happened, the banks would never have believed it possible. Now they could think of nothing else.

What Cleveland Trust and the rest of the banks were really doing in Latin America—quite unbeknown to the credit analysts and loan officers who approved the loans—was funding the greatest financial ripoff in history.

It was a sheer case of private profiteering from the public weal. Evidence for this is provided in the extraordinary gap between the *gross* debt of Latin American countries, and their *net* indebtedness (gross debt minus foreign assets). More than *one third* of the foreign debt of Latin America went to finance the flight of private capital, which means foreign investments by wealthy Latin Americans in New York, Switzerland, or London. Since the debt boom began in 1973, residents of Brazil, Mexico, Argentina, and Venezuela had acquired some $100 billion in overseas assets. That means that they converted their local currencies to dollars and used the money to buy investments abroad. Dollars are not magically generated by their central banks—they are created either by export revenues or by foreign loans, and by far the largest part of those dollars came from foreign loans.

Consider some of the following numbers. In 1980, Argentina borrowed some $9 billion from U.S. and other foreign banks. That same year, Argentines purchased $6.7 billion worth of foreign investments, or *75 percent of the increase in total foreign debt.* The dollars were going out almost as fast as the banks were lending them in.

The same thing happened in Mexico. In 1980, foreign borrowings of $16.4 billion were somehow translated into an increase of $7.1 billion in foreign investments by Mexican nationals. In 1982 it was revealed that the mayor of Mexico City had purchased a $2.5 million estate in Connecticut. It seems he was typical of the wealthy, privileged class of Mexicans who did not trust their economy, so they bought foreign hedges against their own policies. The same year, Brazilian residents, in spite of supposedly strict exchange controls, managed to sneak $1.8 billion out of the country. Venezuela was even more extreme: its residents bought $4.7 billion in foreign assets in a year when the country's total borrowing was only $3.2 billion.

These figures refer only to the original placements of funds, not the growth of those funds. At an annual growth rate of 10 percent, the foreign assets of those countries have already reached a sum in excess of $175 billion, while their gross foreign debt is estimated at some $300 billion. But the banks can't touch that $175 billion, because it doesn't belong to the original borrower. However, it is still owed by the sovereign governments of Brazil, Argentina, Mexico, and Venezuela. The banks have no claims on estates in Connecticut, condos in Palm Springs, U.S. government T-bills, or Eurodollar investments. Their claims are primarily on the governments themselves, who cannot go bankrupt and have no foreign assets left to pay debt.

What this means is that the residents of those countries cynically exploited subsidized exchange rates—often borrowing in cheap local currencies, converting them to dollars, and "exporting" them as investments, never to return.

So it was with most of Latin America. Capital flight had long been common in a country such as Venezuela, where inflations were frequent and virulent, and where much of the economy relied on a single commodity for its well-being. A fall in the price of that commodity, or a run of bad inflation, would endanger accumulated wealth—and so the Venezuelans had traditionally hedged themselves, and their patriotism, with foreign investments. If you wanted to be sure that Junior would be able to go to Harvard, or that your grandson would be able to afford a large house and a fine lifestyle, then you were wise to put your money in trust with a U.S. bank, or in real estate, or at least in a Eurodeposit. It is impossible to argue with this sort of practicality. What would you want your children to be drawing against, pesos or dollars? But the implication is obvious: the Latins never believed in their own economies the way the American banks had been duped into believing in them.

But why had the banks never bothered to check those numbers? Why did it take a study by the Federal Reserve Bank in 1984 to reveal what they should have required all along as evidence of the sincerity of their creditors? The banks were not, as some have suggested, lending in spite of the certain knowledge that their money was landing a few days or months later in a New York bank account under a name that did not appear in the loan agreement. But all of us knew foreign bankers and businessmen with foreign investments. As one of my former clients said, "You'd have to be crazy not to put some of your money offshore." He was right—but the banks were just as crazy to lend it.

For one thing, those numbers were never published anywhere. And if they had been published, they would have been years out of date and easy to dismiss as old news. In any case, it had never occurred to banks to *require* them. In some countries—Brazil is the most notorious—strict foreign exchange controls had been instituted to prevent capital flight. But "strict" turned out to mean only that you had to have connections to be allowed to take your overvalued cruzeiros—worthless on international markets—to the central bank and exchange them for American dollars, thoughtfully provided by Citicorp and Cleveland Trust and others. A client once told me how it worked: If you had connections, you told the central bank that you wanted the dollars to import goods; the connections made sure that no one ever checked to see if you had imported anything; then you used the dollars to buy a permanent, offshore investment in dollars.

Capital flight illustrates one of those obscure twists of the debt crisis, one that is almost never talked about or written about: the fact that most of the Latin American debt never left the United States. When Pedro Mitro made a loan to a Mexican newspaper to buy a printing press from Harris Corporation, he often disbursed the money directly to a U.S. dollar account owned by Harris Corp. Or, if he disbursed the money to the Mexican newspaper's account, then it went quickly over to Harris's account. The money never left the U.S., and usually never even left New York. On the bank's balance sheet, it showed a debit in the form of a cash payment to another U.S. bank, and a credit in the form of a loan to a Mexican company. Similarly, most of Latin America's foreign exchange reserves—again the product of bank loans—were held in dollar accounts either in the U.S. domestic or in the Eurocurrency market. As was shown earlier, all Eurodollars are really housed in American banks. Capital flight itself is something of a misnomer. Dollars loaned to, say, the Brazilian central bank never go anywhere near Brazil. They stay here. And when the central bank allows a Brazilian to trade cruzeiros for dollars to pay for a U.S. export or for a condo in Miami Beach, the proceeds of that transaction appear in a U.S. bank account owned by that Brazilian. Again, the money never leaves. The entire external financial problem of Brazil can be explained in terms of movements of money between American banks.

The pernicious flight of capital was not the only thing the banks did not know about. As the autumn of 1982 rolled on, more and more astounding revelations came forth.

There was the disturbing case of Venezuela, which in September 1982, in order to keep the confidence of foreign banks, had loudly and pub-licly valued the total of its "reserves" against its aggregate debt. By revaluing its gold reserves from $42 an ounce to $300 an ounce and consolidating its foreign reserve holdings, Venezuela jumped its official reserves from $6.1 billion to $17.4 billion. Since it had estimated its foreign debt at $18 billion, Venezuela's currency reserves thus nearly offset its debt, which in any case was tiny when measured against that of Brazil and Mexico.

But later in the fall the country's economic position worsened. A fall in the price of oil knocked its revenues off target, and the credit-cutting activities of the regional and European banks blocked access to billions of short-term dollars. In November, the Venezuelan finance minister suddenly discovered the fact that nearly half of the country's foreign debt—which had not been reported—was in the form of short-term loans. Venezuela's real foreign debt, he said, was more like $35 billion. But even this number was not right. By the time the Venezuelans got around to counting it all up in February 1983, the new number was $43 billion. This meant that every country study done by the international banks prior to that date had been disastrously wrong. The whole affair was reminiscent of Indonesia's debt crisis ten years before, when loan agree-ments for hundreds of millions of dollars had been found lost or hidden in desk drawers, unrecorded, and unknown to the rest of the world.

What the banks did not know thus hurt them badly. But what they did know—and refused to do anything about—was just as dangerous. Brazil, for instance, was the classic example of a country that for years had relied on deficit financing to prop up its economy, using debt to sustain artificially high levels of growth and per capita income. To fi-nance its deficit it had both borrowed abroad and run its printing presses full tilt in order to "monetize" its domestic debt, a form of invisible taxation that led to a Weimar Germany–style inflation in excess of 200 percent a year. The banks had been too busy competing with each other for loans to try to force Brazil into less profligate economics. They certainly could have tried. And if a strong nationalism caused Brazilians to reject their suggestions, they could simply have let Brazil finance its welfare state and rising standard of living out of its own savings, the way America did after the British banks cut off its credit in the 1840s. Teaching borrowers "discipline" and enforcing austerity would later become the role of the IMF. But the IMF would not be summoned until

Brazil's cash coffers were empty, and by then it was too late to do anything about it.

Monetization of debt plays a big part in the international debt crisis, especially in Latin America. Bolivia provides the extreme, but illustrative example of the phenomenon, accurately described in a League of Nations report on the Central European inflations of the 1920s. "Inflation is the form of taxation that even the weakest government can enforce," the report concluded, "when it can enforce nothing else." Bolivia's inflation in January 1985 was running at an annual rate of 116,000 percent. Planeloads of money arrived twice a week just to keep pace with it—enough of it to make money the country's third-largest import.

Brazil had a similar problem, though on a far grander scale. Delfim Netto, architect of Brazil's growth surge in the 1960s and 1970s, had adopted dozens of policies that were guaranteed to produce a great deal of easy credit, a rising standard of living, and annual GNP growth. They were also guaranteed to produce billions of dollars of unrepayable debts.

Take, for example, his "incomes policy," which pegged increases in wages slightly above the inflation rate, itself already over 100 percent in 1979. Indexing kept the employees of the government corporations— the twenty-four largest companies in Brazil—happy. They were made even happier by the fact that they could not be laid off, and that they received sixteen monthly salaries for eleven months' work, retirement at age 50, free or subsidized housing, and health care. In 1979, Delfim decided that he could beat inflation with a successful harvest. So he expanded rural credit, making loans to farmers at one fourth the rate of inflation. The farmers, quite naturally, put most of this money back into the money market, where the rates were pegged to inflation. Norman Gall wrote in *Forbes* magazine that, "According to a World Bank Report, the acreage financed was from 30 percent to 100 percent greater than the area harvested for the main crops—soybeans, wheat, coffee, and sugar."

The Brazilian government had for years been unable to levy taxes to pay for its wasteful state capitalism, so it resorted to borrowing, both domestically and abroad, and to the old ploy of printing money to pay its debt. Cleveland Trust's dollars were being funneled into a chaotic, deficit-ridden system that had to run out of money sooner or later, for the same reasons that had made it grow so fast just a few years before.

All of this is simple economics. Brazil did exactly what Germany had done in the half century prior to World War I, with exactly the same consequences. But the banks noticed only the 7 percent GNP growth in the 1970s, not the financial sleight-of-hand that was generating it. More importantly, they never required any discipline in exchange for their money. They required nothing, in fact, but prompt payment of interest, a practice unheard of in any other form of banking. As in so many other areas of international lending, intense competition led the banks to establish radical and imprudent double standards.

None of the above ever appeared in a Cleveland Trust country study on Latin America, and yet the bank always felt—until the crushing revelations of late 1982—that it had good credit and country information on which to base its loans. I do not mean to single the bank out: nobody spoke of those things, no bank or country intelligence service ran those numbers out for public view. In the go-go years of international lending, no one wanted to look that closely.

3

THE MEETINGS in Ben Bailey's office during the dark months of 1983 had about them a feeling of *fin de siècle* weariness, a sense that the old innocence, the joy of hustling money for profit were gone. For the men and women in those meetings the business of banking was suddenly and strangely unreal, missing all of its old spontaneity. Their Latin loans were not dead, exactly—there were still $195 million worth of them out there, lost in the tangled finances of Mexico, Brazil, and Venezuela. But the numbers came to mean less and less. As professionals, the participants knew that they had been effectively removed from the decision making. Twelve months before they had been money salesmen: now they were highly paid errand boys, creatures of the "big picture" policy decisions that controlled banking in Latin America.

The meetings typically followed one of Mitro's trips to New York, where he and hundreds of other small creditors had been force-fed pedantic wisdom from the restructuring specialists at the big New York banks. The information he retrieved was extraordinarily complex. There was $220 billion at stake in Brazil, Mexico, and Venezuela alone. Thousands of banks, and thousands of borrowers, both public and private, were involved, and all had different concerns, different maturities, and different perceptions of the problem. Offers and counteroffers played across the telex machines of the world financial community—some of them were more than nineteen feet long.

The reason for all this attention to detail was that the banks, while faced with the de facto inability of Latin America to repay the principal on its debt, nonetheless steadfastly refused to accept the idea that they would not continue to receive the interest on that debt. And all of the reschedulings that have taken place since 1982 have been slanted that way. As far as the bankers were concerned, it was Brazil's problem, not theirs, that it owed $10 billion in interest alone that year before it could repay a penny of principal. Thousands of pages of documents, regression analyses, and payment schedules had the sole purpose of maintaining the myth that the loans were still viable. For if they were not, then the banks could not accrue interest on them, and if the banks could not accrue interest, they would collectively lose billions of dollars a year.

What Mitro brought back from New York was thus a *fait accompli*. The meetings were odd, almost contemplative exercises. In the same office where Bailey, Herrick, and Mitro had planned their marketing strategies two years before, a group of men including Bailey, Perelman, and Ted Ramsey, an executive vice-president and the bank's chief credit officer, now listened calmly as Mitro reported the latest news. Bailey would occasionally get up and walk to the candy jar on his corner credenza, choose a piece of candy and then walk slowly back to his desk, while Ramsey chain-smoked and Perelman inquired about the legal aspects of the maneuvers. Even in the earliest meetings it was clear that there was really no role here for Bailey. He was a middle manager in a business which had no more use for middle managers, except as detail men and errand boys. Bailey was a product of the boom years, a salesman, and quite the opposite of a detail man. The new generation of international bankers would be averse to risk; geared to precision, not loan production. As if to confirm this, the meetings were later moved to Ramsey's office on the twenty-sixth floor, where he would meet alone with Mitro and Perelman. It was the beginning of the end for the Latin American area. Herrick had already moved on to Chicago. An assistant vice-president named Becky Brewer, who had worked the area for five years, joined Citibank's new Cleveland office. Mitro would take a job with American Express in 1984. And Bailey would be replaced by Charles Hammel at the turn of the year.

But as the debt crisis began to take its toll on the human lives in the division, it also cut deeply into the bank's bottom line. There were $30.4 million in loans to the private sector—$16.6 in Mexico and $13.8 in Venezuela—frozen in the no-man's-land of finance known as "nonaccrual." Nonaccrual is an accounting term for loans with interest payments more than ninety days in arrears; for a bank it was the next worst thing to a straight write-off. The reason is that nonaccruing loans cost money: they are funded out of the bank's pool of demand deposits, savings deposits, money market funds, and purchased funds. Assuming a conservative 5 percent cost of funds, Cleveland Trust was actually losing $1.5 million a year on its Mexican and Venezuelan loans.

But the wrenching experience of watching its private-sector loans drift into nonaccrual was still not the worst aspect of 1983. That year the bank was forced to make $19 million in additional loans to Latin America, even though there was no chance that any of its previous loans would be paid off in the next decade. According to the *New York Times,* the regionals had been "badgered, bullied, and cajoled" by the big banks and the IMF into making the new loans.

The rationale for the new loans grew out of two separate considerations. The first was a new, and to many regionals horrifying, IMF invention called "conditionality." The concept had first been outlined at the November 1982 IMF meeting, convened to decide what to do about Mexico. Backed by the American authorities, Jacques de Larosière, head of the IMF, made it clear to the banks that they would have to inject massive new capital into Latin America, starting with $10 billion to Mexico. As journalist Darrell Delamaide put it, "Without the new loans, the last thin veil of contractual rectitude would be withdrawn and reveal sovereign bankruptcy in its ugly nakedness." Conditionality meant that you had to keep lending in order to protect the existing bad debt. There is an old bankers' saying for this: "throwing good money after bad."

The second consideration had to do with the banks' concerns for their own profits. In order to keep those loans out of nonaccrual, there would have to be something resembling reasonably current interest payments. As of the end of 1983, Mexico, Brazil, and Venezuela did not have a prayer of keeping current in 1984. So the purpose of the new loans was really to pay the interest on the debt: In effect, the banks were simply disbursing that money to their own accounts. Cleveland Trust's $19 million in new loans guaranteed that most of its portfolio would stay current. The price paid was taking the unprecedented risk of lending to countries which had already proven that they could not manage large amounts of foreign debt.

Imagine that you have run up a $100,000 bill on your credit cards. The annual interest is $18,000, and you cannot afford to pay any of it, let alone think about repaying principal. Imagine then that the bank, in order to save itself from writing off your debt, lends you an additional $18,000, stipulating that you use that money to pay the interest. Your debt now stands at $118,000, and the interest in the following year will be $21,240. The bank lends you that sum as well, and your new debt rises to $139,240, and so on. The bank writes up a tidy profit each year on your loans; meanwhile you have sunk deeper into debt and are not likely to emerge. Carrying the credit card analogy to its logical conclusion, the bank decides, once your principal has hit $200,000, that you really cannot pay it back. So instead of writing it off, the bank rolls all of your debt into a fifteen-year term loan, lowers the rate of interest, and exhorts you to go out and make a lot of money so that you can pay it back. That all sounds very silly and improbable—but it is exactly what happened on a much larger scale in Mexico and Venezuela in 1984.

By the end of 1984, Cleveland Trust had rolled its Mexican loans into fourteen-year maturities and had given the Mexican government yet another $4.9 million. In Venezuela, its nonaccruing loans totaled 87 percent of its loan portfolio. Its aggregate exposure in Latin America came to just over $200 million.

Chapter Nine

THE PHONY END OF THE DEBT CRISIS

1

WHEN CHARLES Hammel replaced Ben Bailey as head of the international division—no small ascendancy, since the stake ran to some $700 million in foreign loans—he inherited the wreckage of what was once one of the bank's most profitable lending areas. The wreckage was now manned by an extremely youthful bunch. Hammel himself was only thirty-six. Most of the new staff were too young to remember the easy excesses of the early years. They had never spoken the old vernacular of international banking—market shares, cold calling strategies, loan quotas, etc.—nor shared the easy colloquy born of golf games, embassy receptions, and dinners at five-star hotels. For the newcomers, the banking lexicon was a frightened, euphemistic dialect that hung on words like "restructured principal payout," "interest adjustment," "peso escrow accounts," "rescheduling," "conditionality," and "nonaccrual."

The numbers in Cleveland Trust's annual report read like a casualty count. The international division's $4,114,000 profit in 1982 had turned into a $560,000 loss in 1983. In 1984, a $4-million write-off of bad private-sector debt in Mexico left it with a thin profit of $341,000 on listed assets of $990,000,000 (which included the bank's Eurodeposit placements)—a return of only .03 percent. And some $200 million was frozen solid in arcane Latin restructuring schemes over which Hammel had no control.

Most of the damage had been done by Latin American borrowers, and because of this the entire Third World had lost favor among the bank's credit committees. They had never trusted it anyway. Since the shock of Mexico's insolvency, Brock Weir and his successor, Jerry Jarrett, had ordered what amounted to a full-scale retreat from the earth's high-risk regions. They had been burned in Poland, scared to death in the Philippines, and hog-tied in Mexico, Brazil, and Venezuela. They would try not to let this happen again. Term loans and trade financings were slashed by $130 million, as Bailey and then Hammel undertook to pull out from the Third World. Simultaneously, the division began to move its loans en masse—some $407 million—into supersafe, short-term bank loans in Japan and the United Kingdom. A portfolio once top-heavy with Third World debt was now top-heavy with credits to mature, industrialized economies. Regional banks across America were all doing the same thing.

The domestic bank was having its troubles too. After ten consecutive years of increase, its net income dropped from $60 million in 1981 to $56 million in 1982, and again in 1983 to $51 million. The bank's assets had virtually stopped growing. In just five years, Cleveland Trust had fallen from first to fourth in total assets among Ohio's banks, and Weir and Jarrett had missed out on several big in-state bank acquisitions. To make matters worse, the bank had an uncomfortably high percentage of nonperforming loans to companies in the Midwest, where the recession had cut deeply. In a belated effort to streamline itself, it had initiated early retirement programs and hiring freezes, such that between 1980 and 1983—while the rest of the banking industry was rapidly expanding—the number of employees actually shrunk by 580. There were plans under way to cut personnel by another 10 percent.

Seen from this angle, one would expect that Wall Street would have turned its cold eye on Cleveland Trust and forced the price of its stock down, the way it had reduced the share prices of Bank of America, Citicorp, Manufacturers Hanover, Chase Manhattan, and others whose price/earnings multiples had fallen from 4.5 to 3.5 in spite of overall earnings growth.

But here the story takes a startling turn. At the end of 1981, after ten years of earnings growth and an almost flawless international lending record, Cleveland Trust's stock was trading at $30.25 a share. By December 31, 1982, the year its earnings dropped by $4 million, and the year it found itself mired in the Latin debt swamp, the price of its stock *rose 18 percent* to $35.75. In 1983, while income was taking an abrupt 12.5 percent dive, and millions of dollars of foreign loans had either been rescheduled or placed in nonaccrual, Cleveland Trust's stock, beyond any reasonable prediction, rocketed to $48.50 a share. And on December 31, 1984, it hit $57.63 a share.

This was not a Wall Street pipe dream. In 1984 Cleveland Trust's earnings jumped $19 million to hit a historical high of $70,366,000, in spite of the $4 million in international write-offs. That year it acquired an 88 percent interest in Colorado's fifth largest bank, the $2-billion Central Bancorporation. Since 1983 it had been attracting hundreds of millions of dollars in new corporate CDs—refugees from the money center banks—and was referred to in the *Wall Street Journal* as a "rock solid" regional bank. By mid-1985, the bank again resembled the formidable heartland juggernaut it had been for most of the century. The state of its international finances seemed to make no difference at all.

2

THERE WERE two reasons for Wall Street's peculiar vote of confidence. The first had to do with the practice of leveraging.

In the years leading up to the debt crisis, Cleveland Trust's balance sheet had been something of a curiosity to the bigger, more aggressive banks, who regarded it as a colorful anachronism, the product of a management that refused to accommodate itself to the Wild West ethos of the new international banking set. Throughout the 1970s, while the money center banks were using the Euromarket to leverage themselves 20 or 25 to 1, Brock Weir had stuck resolutely to the same 10 to 1 assets-to-capital ratio the bank had had in 1920. When I traveled overseas for the bank, I would try to sell this idea: strongest capital ratio among the top thirty banks, best return on average assets of the top fifty banks, and so on. But this was a strange idea to try to sell in the new world of banking, which did not give a damn about anything but return on equity. Citibankers would simply smile patronizingly and ask what sort of return our shareholders were getting. The answer, naturally, was that

Cleveland Trust had one of the lowest returns on equity of any of the bigger banks, precisely because it had too much capital and too few assets. The easiest way to boost that return was by leveraging yourself. Leverage was safe, everyone said, and it was easy—all you had to do was dial up the Euromarket and ask.

The leverage formula was simple. If you had $1 in capital supporting $10 in loans, you stood to make less money for your shareholders than if that same dollar were supporting $20 or $30 in loans. As long as the loans were good—this was the critical assumption of the Euromarket— the arithmetic was simple and conclusive. There was another benefit: Banks that were leveraged 25 to 1 could, and did, charge half of what Cleveland Trust charged in interest and still make a higher return on equity. The more you leveraged yourself, the more you could indulge yourself in cut-rate lending, and still justify it on your bottom line. For a big bank—and Cleveland Trust qualified as such—a 10 to 1 leverage was considered stodgy and archaic. Who would choose to make five cents on the dollar when he could make an easy 10 cents? In the 1978–1981 period, most of us in the division were deeply envious of the bigger banks' leverage ratios; we agreed that we could go at least another five points in the ratio without causing a scandal. That would have meant another half billion or so in loans, and greater glory for us. Like everyone else in our age and place, we yearned to be more like Citibankers.

But when the hammer came down in 1982 and 1983, all of that changed. The leverage principle had backfired on the money center banks and many smaller Eurobanks that had employed tiny amounts of capital to make large loans. Manufacturers Hanover Trust was discovered to have 260 percent of its equity in loans to Latin America, and some 40 percent to Argentina alone. The numbers at the other money center banks were equally frightening: Citicorp had 179 percent of capital out in Latin America, Bank of America 133 percent, Chase 170 percent, and Chemical 193 percent.

And quite suddenly Brock Weir looked like a genius. The money center banks had made so many loans in Latin America and in the rest of the Third World that Cleveland Trust, with its $200 million in frozen loans against some $600 million in capital, looked positively visionary. As it became more and more difficult to find a big bank that did not have a large percentage of its capital sunk in Third World debt, Wall Street and foreign depositors and investors had come to look favorably on the mid-sized regional that had played it conservatively. Now capital as a percentage of foreign loans was a critical figure. It was one of the reasons that a number of Kuwaitis, for example (large traditional sources of deposits for the money center banks), began to move funds to the regionals. It was the reason Cleveland Trust was inundated in 1983 and 1984 with CDs that had fled from the money centers.

Behind all of this jumpiness about capital ratios was the grim specter of a sovereign repudiation of debt. China, Russia, Cuba, and North Korea had done it in this century. It was not hard to imagine a leftist regime coming to power in Brazil, for example—the political product of the austerity imposed by $90 billion in foreign debt—a regime that might well choose to absolve itself of the sins of its military predecessors. Such a repudiation would devour most of Citibank's capital, and probably destroy it outright. It was impossible to dismiss that potential.

But that was only one reason for Wall Street's confidence in Cleveland Trust. The other was the undeniable fact that although the bank had millions in nonaccruing loans to private sector borrowers in Mexico and Venezuela, fully $170 million of that $200 million was accruing interest at market rates. This aspect of the debt crisis—the continuing high bank profits—is often overlooked. The defaults and reschedulings did more than just frighten the financial world. It also meant billions of dollars of profits to the banks. You could look at Cleveland Trust two ways: as a bank trapped against its will in foreign debt markets; or as a bank that was guaranteed high rates and fees for the next fifteen years on a $170-million loan portfolio.

From the bankers' point of view, interest is the key to the debt crisis. Interest is in part what caused it in the first place; interest is what all of the elaborate machinations and restructurings are all about.

Lending money to a debtor so that the debtor can pay interest on his loan is a good idea if your business is loan sharking, and if you have plenty of muscle to see that the interest, and ultimately the principal, gets paid. For a bank, it is suicidal. U.S. banks had been doing it long before the debt crisis began in August 1982. Between 1977 and 1983, Latin America's foreign debt increased from $116 billion to $336 billion. What is interesting about this is that of the $220-billion rise in debt, $154 billion was eaten up by *interest payments on past debt*. From 1977 to 1979, Brazil's debt rose by $16 billion, while it paid over $11 billion of that back to the banks in the form of interest. Mexico borrowed $60 billion between 1977 and 1982, of which $43 billion went to pay interest. Argentina borrowed $32 billion between 1977 and 1983 and paid $19 billion in interest. None of this was quite as neat as the numbers make it sound. The debt and interest figures represent the *aggregate* external debt position, while the actual loans and interest payments involved many different government and private-sector borrowers. But as we have seen, in a world where pesos, zlotys, bolivars and cruzeiros cannot settle international debt, the aggregate numbers never lie.

Lending to pay interest is not productive lending. It is either the act of an extremely powerful creditor—the loan shark—or of an immensely weak one, whose very existence is threatened by the fact that he is paying the interest on that loan himself.

Why did the banks agree to that? Because their own money markets had gone crazy in the late 1970s and early 1980s, doubling the interest rates foreign borrowers had to pay. The price of oil had tripled again, and debtors were suddenly looking at an income-outgo picture they had never been prepared for. The way out of those straits was obviously—or so it seemed—through robust economic growth, and that was the spirit of many of those loans. But no such effect was ever produced. Big U.S. banks could see only their particular loans to particular borrowers: money for a hydroelectric plant, or funds to be lent to other parties through a development bank. Had they chosen to look at the economy as a whole, they would have seen that their money was really going to finance capital flight and interest payments, neither of which was generating a single cent of GNP growth.

By the early 1980s, interest had become a terrible burden and had placed the fate of the Third World in the grasp of the money markets. A 1 percent rise in the U.S. prime rate meant another billion or so dollars a year in interest for Mexico and Brazil. There are only two ways to make enough money to keep current: one is by exporting, the other is by borrowing. The former has not worked. The 1983 trade surplus for all of Latin America, for example, was $25 billion, against $38 billion in interest payments. Brazil's $6.3-billion trade surplus fell $5.2 billion short of its interest payments that year. Argentina fell $3.5 billion short. Mexico alone broke even. But what did Mexico gain by doing so? It meant only that the country did not have to go more deeply in debt just to service existing debt. But not a penny of its $90 billion in principal had been touched, and virtually nothing was left over to build foreign reserves or to finance increased domestic investment, which is what Mexico needs in the long run to make itself solvent again. And in the meantime domestic austerity was becoming a very bitter pill for an increasingly poor population to swallow.

On February 4, 1985, the *New York Times* ran a headline that read "Debt Crisis Called All But Over," in which several bankers were quoted saying how pleased they were about their new agreement with Argentina, the country that had just won an extended game of chicken with them and the IMF over repayment terms. Argentina had refused for more than a year to cooperate with the banks, rejecting their terms, demanding domestic economic freedom and a long, leisurely repayment. In spite of their high rhetoric, threats, and claims that "cooperative" countries like Mexico and Venezuela would receive better terms than the prodigals, the banks finally caved in to Argentina and gave it an even more lenient package than they had given Mexico the summer before. All of which proved to the world that the banks had never had any bargaining position in the first place. They never had a choice: If they refused to allow Argentina more time to pay off and more money in the meantime, they would have to declare default and take an excruciating blow to their earnings.

Yet there they were in the *New York Times,* calling the debt crisis "over," claiming that the worst of the storm had been weathered. It was a peculiar bit of public relations. What had really happened was that Argentina, $1 billion behind on its interest payments and $10 billion behind on principal, had backed the banks up against the wall. It had virtually dictated repayment terms and refused many of the IMF's demands for economic austerity. The only major concession it had granted the banks was *continued repayment of interest at market rates.* This was what they were really crowing about in the *Times.* What made it even more ridiculous was that their single point of victory, market-rate interest, is itself the largest threat to the economic viability of Latin America in the 1980s and 1990s.

As for the debt crisis being over, it became quickly apparent that this was not the case, at least not in Argentina. In May 1985, inflation was raging at over 1,000 percent, its financial industry was collapsing, and dozens of banks were failing or in deep trouble. Amid rumors of a nationalization of the banks, the stocks of the money center banks in the U.S. took an abrupt dive on May 24. The bankers, apparently, were the only ones who thought they were out of the woods.

3

I HAVE said that lending to pay interest is more properly the domain of loan sharks than of commercial banks. When a loan has deteriorated so far that the borrower can no longer even meet the interest, you've got to get a tough, insensitive goon to go out and protect that new money. Since the Polish crisis, the banks have found such a goon—a powerful bringer of bad tidings to the embattled Third World called the International Monetary Fund. The banks could not be happier about their discovery. "The IMF," wrote Karin Lissakers in *Foreign Policy*, "is acting as enforcer of the banks' loan contracts because continued access to IMF funds is contingent upon the debtor's regular payments on its commercial interest." According to Brazilian economist Paul Singer, "The power of the IMF is absolute. No foreign country can get a single cent without an extended agreement from it."

The IMF is an international agency composed of 146 member nations, almost every one of them outside the Soviet bloc. The membership dues consist of portions of foreign currency reserves earmarked for the IMF, each nation's quota being determined by the size of a country's economy and its participation in world trade. The U.S. holds by far the largest quota at $19.2 billion.

The money to pay the IMF comes from taxes, naturally, and the $8.4-billion 1984 increase in the U.S. quota came under attack from both the left and the right, uniting such strange bedfellows as Jesse Helms and Ralph Nader. The debate pivoted around the idea of lending to pay interest—often interest that itself was incurred by lending to pay interest. The IMF's new role is both as lender and fiscal policeman. In each of the recent bailouts of Latin American countries, the IMF has participated with its own funds—and has required the banks to participate too. The problem is that all of the new loans are being funneled directly to the banks themselves as interest income. Which means that our tax money is being used to repay bankers who have made ten years' worth of egregious lending errors in the Third World.

Along with interest came the "fees." In exchange for conditionality, the U.S. banks have been allowed to charge rescheduling fees, which, instead of being applied to reduce principal, again went directly to their bottom lines. With their market rates and fees intact, it was reminiscent of the good old days in the late 1970s, except that now they had the IMF, a kind of global FDIC, watching over their loans and fattening them with U.S. tax dollars.

The banks have also, by the good graces of the Federal Reserve Bank and the U.S. Treasury—which have been pushing cooperation with the IMF all along—been allowed to engage in what were previously considered unconscionable banking practices. Regulators have tolerated their practice of understating the risk of their loan portfolios; they have not required the banks to build reserves against losses; they have permitted billions of dollars of what ought to be nonaccruing loans to accrue interest at profitable spreads over LIBOR; they have permitted the banks to lend in order to pay themselves interest, without using any of the money to amortize principal. U.S. regulators have also allowed them to stretch the legal lending limit—normally 15 percent of capital or a federally chartered bank—to make new loans to troubled debtors.

This neat arrangement whereby you and I give money to the U.S. government, which gives it to the IMF, which lends it to pay bank interest on loans that should be reclassified, has been termed a "Faustian bargain." Even Federal Reserve Board Chairman Paul Volcker admitted, "We're all being induced to close our eyes to loose banking practices."

The problem with all this is that it serves to maintain the illusion that market interest is perfectly compatible with the well-being of Third World debtors. It ignores the simple fact that the interest burden is ruining the sovereign economies south of the border. According to the January 1985 report of the Council of the Americas, "Under current circumstances, officials estimate that it will take until the end of the decade for per capita growth to return to pre-debt crisis levels." Per capita income has fallen 20 percent since 1982 and will decline for the rest of the decade. "International bankers," wrote New York Congressman Charles E. Schumer and economist Alfred J. Watkins in the *New Republic*, "are now betting that virtually all of Latin America will tolerate a decade of economic stagnation and decay simply so that their bankers can earn market rates of interest on debt that was contracted years ago to pay earlier rounds of interest."

There is no easy solution to the debt crisis. Too much money is involved to simply wipe the slate clean, and anything short of that necessarily involves thousands of principals with much at stake. But there is a logical first step, and that is for the banks to give up as quickly as possible the misguided notion that they can earn market interest on this debt. They should be prohibited from lending money to pay themselves interest. Instead, they should be required to use those loans—and the restructuring fees they receive—to amortize principal, because that is the only way Latin America is every going to be able to pull itself up. Interest must be reduced in two ways.

First, there should be a "cap"—something the banks have resisted with fierce hostility—on the base rate of interest charged to the borrowers. That means that should LIBOR rise again to 20 percent, the banks would incur losses, since they would be paying more for their funds than they were receiving in interest. This is as it should be. If Latin governments erred in taking on the debt, then so did the commercial banks err in lending out so indiscriminately. Interest risk should be shared.

Second, the actual spread over LIBOR—what the banks actually make—should be substantially reduced. All of this would mean that the banks will take an "earnings hit": their stocks will fall again, they will not be as profitable for at least the next two decades. But this is a far more appealing alternative than simply waiting for the debt bomb—in the form of social revolution, debt repudiation, and the rest—to go off. None of this would solve the crisis, but it would be an important first step in establishing reasonable terms for Latin America to bail itself out.

4

IN MY travels for Cleveland Trust in Asia and in the Middle East, it was impossible to avoid the impression that we were just dilettantes in the world of international finance. I could make loans for the bank, and even earn lots of interest income. In those days it was not hard for an institution with money to find someone to take it. But I always had the feeling that we were way outside the corridors of real power. Visiting a Citicorp branch in Taiwan, or Hong Kong, or the Philippines was an awe-inspiring experience. They owned real estate, they typically received billions of dollars in Euroinvestments from national treasuries. They often ran "clearing" operations in the U.S. for the governments and central banks of foreign countries; which meant, in effect, that all payments in the U.S. would run through accounts at Citibank. This meant tens of millions of dollars in demand deposits, which the banks did not have to pay for—another reason Citibank could always afford to be a cut-rate lender. In Hong Kong alone the bank owned a sky-scraper and employed thousands of people, both Chinese and American. In Brazil, where Citibank typically earned some 20 percent of its total income, it owned even more real estate, more banks, employed more people, and had even more profitable clearing operations.

Citibank—and the other big U.S. banks—had built huge stakes over-seas in the 1960s and 1970s, while most of the regionals, like Cleveland Trust, had not. Their loans as a percentage of capital were often triple or quadruple those of the big regionals. And when the debt crisis hap-pened, it was the money center banks, not the regionals, that were left holding the bag. Their stakes were such that they could not, as Cleve-land Trust could, walk away from the debt.

All of this has created a tension between the money center banks and the regionals on the subject of refinancing foreign debt—a growing ten-sion which poses a major threat to the carefully calculated restructuring schemes of the last three years.

As of December 31, 1983, the money center banks accounted for 60 percent of U.S. bank loans in Latin America and the Caribbean. But in the first half of 1984, they came up with *83 percent* of the new money. In spite of their browbeating of the smaller banks, they—who can least afford to do so—are shouldering more and more of the burden.

The regionals, quite simply, are pulling out. The 188 regionals active in international finance reduced their overseas loans by $11 billion in the first six months of 1984, while the money center banks held even at $207 billion. Providence's Fleet Bank, for example, has reduced its for-eign exposure by 25 percent since 1982, in part by not rolling over its Latin loans when they came due. Other regionals have either refused outright to make any new loans, or have traded their foreign loans for domestic loans. To keep Latin America afloat the banks will almost certainly have to make fresh loans over the next ten years. The big banks will be able to count less and less on the regionals to help with the financing, which means that ever greater proportions of the big banks' capital will be tied up. At the same time, the regionals will have less and less at stake, and therefore even less reason than they have now to cooperate. Last year Cleveland Trust made a profit of $70 million dol-lars, almost entirely off domestic banking where it has invested millions over the last decade to improve its retail and commercial services. A write-off of its Mexican debt—all $116 million of it—would be a hard but sustainable blow. The bank would recover quickly and would probably be even stronger when it came back, especially relative to the larger banks which will inevitably sink deeper in the debt hole. A write-off of such debt would also have the effect of persuading other regionals to do the same, and that would almost certainly lead us into the next great crisis cycle, from which many of the big banks may not emerge intact.

APPENDIX

THE FOLLOWING table is a random sample of the foreign lending activities of some of the larger regional banks. Taken individually, they cannot match the power of a Citibank or a Manufacturers Hanover. Viewed in aggregate, though, one begins to realize their importance. Note that there is not a single money center bank on the list, and that the banks that do appear are but representatives of America's top 150 banks, most of which have international credits outstanding.

The figures were taken from the banks' 1983 annual reports.

CROSS-BORDER RISK OF SELECTED REGIONAL U.S. BANKS AT 12/31/83

Bank	Total Assets	Foreign Loans & Deposits
	(BILLIONS)	(MILLIONS)
Society National Bank (Ohio)	$4.3	$68
National City Corp. (Ohio)	$6.6	$237
Union Bank (Calif.)	$7.9	$715
North Carolina National Bank (NCNB)	$12.2	$2,127
Mellon National Corp. (Pittsburgh)	$20.3	$3,542
Seafirst Corp. (Washington)	$8.5	$972
Centerre (St. Louis)	$5.4	$207
Marine Corp. (Wisconsin)	$2.5	$69
First Wisconsin Corp.	$5.1	$723
Interfirst (Dallas)	$21.8	$926
First City Bancorp of Texas	$17.2	$1,088
Connecticut Bank and Trust (CBT)	$5.8	$871
Bank of New England Corp. (Massachusetts)	$5.8	$448
Southwest Bancshares (Texas)	$8.0	$439
First Bank System (Minnesota)	$20.8	$3,529
First Pennsylvania	$5.2	$831
Maryland National Corp.	$5.7	$890
Pittsburgh National Corp. (PNC)	$12.2	$2,344
Wachovia Corp. (North Carolina)	$7.9	$1,102
Bancal Tri-State Corp. (Bank of California)	$3.9	$1,065
United Virginia Bankshares	$5.4	$253
Rainier Bancorp (Washington)	$6.4	$1,105
Total	$198.9	$23,551

NOTES

CHAPTER 1: *Whistling Past the Graveyard*

PAGE

14 THE WORLD'S LARGEST BANKS: S. I. Davis, *The Euro-Bank: Its Origins, Management, and Outlook* (New York: John Wiley and Sons, Halstead Press, 1976), Chapter 2.

14 THE HOPELESSLY WEAK PESO: Howard Rudnitsky, "Why Manana Came Early," *Forbes*, March 15, 1982.

14 INTO THE COUNTRY: Penny Lernoux, *In Banks We Trust* (advance uncorrected proofs) (Garden City, N.Y.: Anchor/Doubleday, 1983), p. 231.

15 IN FOREIGN LOANS: Karin Lissakers, "Dateline Wall Street: Faustian Finance," *Foreign Policy*, Fall 1983, p. 160.

16 A DECADE BEFORE: John Brooks, *The Go-Go Years* (New York: E. P. Dutton, 1984), p. 211.

17 THE LENDER AT ALL: Karl Marx, *Capital: A Critique of Political Economy* (New York: Modern Library, 1932), p. 284.

20 "ESCAPE INTO MAKE-BELIEVE": J. K. Galbraith, *The Great Crash—1929* (Boston: Houghton Mifflin, 1955).

PAGE

21 $400 BILLION OF FOREIGN DEBT: Lawrence Rout, "Postponement of Third World Debt Threatens Upheaval, Financial Collapse," *Wall Street Journal*, June 22, 1984, p. 29.

22 CHEMICAL BANK, $1.4 BILLION: "Argentine Debt Pact Avoids Trouble Now, May Cause Pain Later," *Wall Street Journal*, News Roundup, April 2, 1984. (Figures are from 12/31/84.)

23 $48 BILLION TO U.S. BANKS: Alan Riding, "Mexican Outlook: Banks Are Wary," *New York Times*, August 17, 1982.

24 CLEVELAND TRUST'S BRANCHES: This story has been circulating in Cleveland for many years and is repeated proudly by Cleveland Trust executives to clients. Whether true or not, it constitutes part of the legend of the bank.

24 TO LATIN AMERICAN COUNTRIES: Rick Rieff, "Banks Uneasy over Latin Loans," *Akron Beacon Journal*, June 4, 1984.

25 THE GAME WAS ALREADY UP: Rout, "Postponement of Third World Debt."

25 TURN OF THE YEAR: Rudnitsky,"Why Manana Came Early."

The chronology of events contained in section 4 was derived mainly from accounts in the *Wall Street Journal* and the *New York Times* during the weeks of August 13 and August 20, 1982.

CHAPTER 2: *Into the Money Vortex*

PAGE

28 FOR WORLD TRADE: Michael Moffitt, *The World's Money: International Banking from Bretton Woods to the Brink of Insolvency* (New York: Touchstone Books, 1984), p. 67.

28 AND DOCUMENTARY CREDITS: *Cleveland Trust Annual Report, 1978.*

29 "AS REMOTE AS THE MOON": Anthony Sampson, *The Money Lenders* (New York: Viking Press, 1981), p. 115.

30 "A CROWD OF MEN": Max Beerbohm, *Zuleika Dobson.*

31 ONE-TRILLION-DOLLAR MONEY VORTEX: Moffitt, *The World's Money*, p. 66.

36 PATRON OF THE RENAISSANCE: S. I. Davis, *The Euro-Bank: Its Origins, Management, and Outlook* (New York: John Wiley and Sons, Halstead Press, 1976), pp. 7–8.

39 BANK IN AMERICA: *Cleveland Trust Annual Report, 1945.*

39 SECOND BANK OF THE UNITED STATES: Carter H. Golembe, "The Changing Character of Banking," in *The Changing World of Banking*, ed. Herbert V. Prochnow and Herbert V. Prochnow, Jr. (New York: Harper & Row, 1974), pp. 15–16. Also, Bray Hammond, *Banks and Politics in America* (Princeton, N.J.: Princeton University Press, 1957), p. 359.

39 COMMERCIAL BANKS IN THE UNITED STATES: Golembe, "The Changing Character of Banking," p. 19.

39 RECESSION OF THE 1930S: Penny Lernoux, *In Banks We Trust* (advance uncorrected proofs) (Garden City, N.Y.: Anchor/Doubleday, 1983), p. 251.

39 ANYWHERE IN THE STATE: Golembe, "The Changing Character of Banking," p. 20.

PAGE

40 THE MODERN BUSINESS WORLD: *Cleveland Trust Annual Report, 1966*, remarks by Chairman George Gund.

43 ITS EURODOLLAR LOANS: *Cleveland Trust Annual Report, 1973*.

Facts and figures relating to Charles Hammel's expenses, salary, and so forth are estimates based on my own travels and my travels with Hammel from 1979–1981, and on an actual loan to Bank Leumi, Tel Aviv.

CHAPTER 3: *"The Paradise of Little Fat Men"*

PAGE

45 "EXEMPT FROM HISTORY": Darrell Delamaide, *Debt Shock: The Full Story of the World Credit Crisis* (Garden City, N.Y.: Anchor/Doubleday, 1984), p. 16.

46 "WONDERFULLY RIGHT": M. S. Mendelsohn, *Money on the Move* (New York: McGraw-Hill, 1980), p. 123.

47 THE QUEEN OF DENMARK HAD DIED: Joseph Wechsberg, *The Merchant Bankers* (Boston: Little, Brown, 1966), p. 47.

47 "THIS EARTH IN MINUTES": Walter Wriston, *Global Financial Intermediation* (New York: Citibank, 1980), p. 7.

48 THIRD WORLD IN 1978: Michael Moffitt, *The World's Money: International Banking from Bretton Woods to the Brink of Insolvency* (New York: Touchstone Books, 1984), p. 66.

49 NOTHING WENT REALLY WRONG: George Orwell, *Wigan Pier* (New York: Berkley Medallion Books, 1967), p. 161.

49 $67 BILLION IN 1980: Moffitt, *The World's Money*, p. 107.

49 SHOT THROUGH 20 PERCENT: Ibid., pp. 174–80.

50 BASIC MONETARIST PRINCIPLES: "Chile: A Survey," *Euromoney*, July 1978, p. 21.

50 EMPHATICALLY DID NOT NEED: Delamaide, *Debt Shock*, p. 63.

51 CONFIDENCE IN PERU: Moffitt, *The World's Money*, p. 124.

51 "SKIRTS OF THE IMF": Ibid., p. 125.

52 DEMAND AT HOME: M. van den Adel, "A Burst of Credits," *Euromoney*, March 1978, p. 54.

52 NON-OPEC THIRD WORLD COUNTRIES: Kurt Richolt, "The Eurocredit Market: Between Scylla and Charybdis," *Euromoney*, March 1978, p. 50.

52 MONEY AT ¾ PERCENT: "Buddy Can You Borrow a Dollar?," *Euromoney*, May 1978, p. 10.

53 "KEEP ON LENDING": Quek Pek Lim, "Hectic Year of Borrowing," *Euromoney*, January 1978, p. 14.

53 PAYMENT IN FULL: van den Adel, "A Burst of Credits."

53 $225 BILLION IN ASSETS: James C. Baker, *International Bank Regulation* (New York: Praeger, 1978), pp. 2–3.

53 TOTAL EARNINGS: Mendelsohn, *Money on the Move*, p. 6.

65 DEBT WAS RISING: Norman Gall, "Games Bankers Play," *Forbes*, December 5, 1983, p. 184.

PAGE

66 TIME LAG: Delamaide, *Debt Shock*, p. 50.

66 "IN INTERNATIONAL LOANS": Ibid., p. 51.

66 BOTH BRAZIL AND MEXICO: *Latin America Weekly Report*, December 17, 1982, p. 1.

67 THE NACIONAL FINANCIERA: Ibid., June 18, 1982, p. 6.

67 A PUBLIC GUARANTEE: P. Henry Mueller, "A Conspectus for Offshore Lenders," in *Offshore Lending by U.S. Commercial Banks*, ed. F. John Mathis, Bankers Association for Foreign Trade and Robert Morris Associates, 1975, p. 38.

67 "LARGER THAN SUPPOSED": Mendelsohn, *Money on the Move*, p. 108.

68 $100 BILLION WITH ITSELF: Vivian Brownstein, "The World's Missing Billions," *Fortune*, August 23, 1983, p. 154.

68 "BY EVERY COUNTRY": Ibid.

68 "FOREIGN CURRENCY HOLDINGS": "The Third Brazil," *The Nation*, November 6, 1982, p. 452.

69 FROM 1978 TO 1982: Eduardo Gallardo, "Debtor Nations Wonder Where the Money Went," *Cleveland Plain Dealer*, August 12, 1984.

69 RISK ANALYSIS PROGRAMS: Richard S. Weinert, "Why the Banks Did It," *Foreign Policy*, Spring 1978, p. 143.

70 "OFFER ATTRACTIVE INCENTIVES": Benjamin Weiner, "The Banks Should Have Known Better," *New York Times*, December 19, 1982, sec. 3, p. 2.

70 "TO ADDED INVESTMENT": Ibid.

70 "TALK TO BANK OF AMERICA": Ibid.

71 "BE RELATIVELY FAVOURABLE": *Bank of London and South America Review*, November 1982, p. 158 (a Lloyds Bank Group publication).

73 TO SECURITY ANALYSTS: Mueller, "A Conspectus for Offshore Lenders," p. 19.

73 "IN THE UNITED STATES": J. E. Connor, "Accounting Practices," in *Offshore Lending by U.S. Commercial Banks*, p. 57.

74 "LIKE AMERICAN STATEMENTS": Mario Shao, "Banks Cautious After Taiwan Loan Losses," *Wall Street Journal*, November 7, 1984.

CHAPTER 4: *The Invisible Bank*

PAGE

80 ANY CREDIT ACTIVITY: Background sources on the Euromarkets: Paul Einzig, *Foreign Dollar Loans in Europe* (New York: St. Martin's Press, 1965); Einzig, *The Eurodollar System* (London: Macmillan, 1964); Herbert V. Prochnow and Herbert V. Prochnow, Jr., eds., *The Changing World of Banking* (New York: Harper & Row, 1974); Brian Scott Quinn, *The New Euromarkets* (New York: John Wiley and Sons, Halstead Press, 1975); Daniel R. Kane, *The Eurodollar Market and the Years of Crisis* (New York: St. Martin's Press, 1983); S. I. Davis, *The Euro-Bank* (New York: John Wiley and Sons, Halstead Press, 1976); and M. S. Mendelsohn, *Money on the Move: Its Origins, Management, and Outlook* (New York: McGraw-Hill, 1980).

80 DOUBLED AGAIN IN 1960: Anthony Sampson, *The Money Lenders* (New York: Viking Press, 1981), p. 111.

PAGE

80 "THE NEW PRACTICE": Einzig, *Foreign Dollar Loans in Europe,* p. vi.

81 "BY AMERICAN BANKS": Mendelsohn, *Money on the Move,* p. 24.

82 APPROXIMATELY $75 BILLION: Davis, *The Euro-Bank,* p. 29, and Sampson, *The Money Lenders,* p. 228.

85 IN THE SAME PERIOD: From *Cleveland Trust Annual Reports* and Forms 10-K.

86 CONSISTS OF INTERBANK DEPOSITS: Michael Moffitt, *The World's Money: International Banking from Bretton Woods to the Brink of Insolvency* (New York: Touchstone Books, 1984), p. 69.

87 NEARLY $10 BILLION: Jeff Bailey and G. Christian Hill, "Continental Illinois' Future Depends on Merger," *Wall Street Journal,* May 25, 1984.

87 "WILD LACK OF CONTROL": Ibid.

87 THEIR LONG-TERM LOANS: Daniel R. Kane, *The Eurodollar Market and the Years of Crisis,* Chapter 3.

87 ROSE BY ONLY 71 PERCENT: Lee Berton, "Long Before Run at Continental Illinois, Bank Hinted at Ills," *Wall Street Journal,* July 12, 1984.

88 MINIMUM OF STOCK COLLATERAL: See J. K. Galbraith's account of the investment trusts in *The Great Crash—1929* (Boston: Houghton Mifflin, 1955).

88 COMFORTABLY UNDER 10 TO 1: Friedrich Engels, Introduction to Karl Marx, *Capital: A Critique of Political Economy* (New York: Modern Library, 1932), p. iii.

88 TO BE INORDINATELY HIGH: Davis, *The Euro-Bank,* pp. 87–88.

88 THE TOP TEN BANKS: "Banks Act to Minimize Risk," *Wall Street Journal,* October 15, 1984.

88 FORTY-SIX SUCH ENTITIES: Davis, *The Euro-Bank,* p. 45.

89 "APPROACH TO BANKING": "Anatomy of a Failure," *Wall Street Journal,* July 30, 1984.

90 DOMESTIC MONEY MARKETS: Ibid.

90 $28.3 BILLION IN DEPOSITS: "Problems Continental Illinois Rescue Is Creating," *Business Week,* June 4, 1984, p. 108.

90 CORPORATIONS FELL INTO RANK: Bailey and Hill, "Continental Illinois' Future Depends on Merger."

90 CONTINENTAL'S OFFSHORE BRANCHES: "Banker Uncle Sam," *Wall Street Journal,* July 19, 1984.

92 THE BANKS GOT THEIR CUT: Quinn, *The New Euromarkets,* Chapter 4.

CHAPTER 5: *Cakewalk*

PAGE

97 "ACCORDING TO HER JUDGMENT": Mark Twain, "Is Shakespeare Dead?," in *Complete Essays of Mark Twain,* ed. Charles Neider (Garden City, N.Y.: Anchor/Doubleday, 1963).

97 BUSINESS WITH CHASE: Anthony Sampson, *The Money Lenders* (New York: Viking Press, 1981), pp. 233–43.

98 AGAINST OTHER CURRENCIES: Brendan Brown, *Money Hard and Soft* (New York: John Wiley and Sons, 1978), p. 6.

PAGE

99 AT THE OFFICIAL RATE: International Reports, Inc., *Statistical Market Letter*, June 10, 1977.

101 CARTERET, NEW JERSEY: S. J. Perelman, *Westward Ha!* (New York: Simon & Schuster, 1948), p. 47.

101 A SEVERE HOUSING CRISIS: Jonathan C. Randal, "Algiers Mixes Theories to Straighten Out Economy," *Cleveland Plain Dealer*, August 9, 1984.

101 A MILLION TONS OF CRUDE OIL: Konrad Schliephake, *Oil and Regional Development* (New York: Praeger, 1977), and Randal, "Algiers Mixes Theories."

101 MASSIVE WORKER ABSENTEEISM: Randal, "Algiers Mixes Theories."

101 RAN DEFICITS: Paul Lewis, "Algiers Strives to Halt Waste," *New York Times*, April 20, 1980, p. 5.

102 $1 BILLION A YEAR: John P. Entellis, "Algeria, Myth and Reality," *New York Times*, February 1, 1979.

102 $15 BILLION IN 1979: "World Debt Tables—1979," World Bank.

104 BETWEEN 1977 AND 1982: Robert P. McDonald, *International Syndicated Loans* (London: Euromoney Publications, 1982), p. 65.

105 QUITE LIKE THIS ONE: Ibid., p. 67.

108 "DELINEATED BY GEOGRAPHY": Ibid., p. 38.

108 BANKHAUS I.D. HERSTATT: Sampson, *The Money Lenders*, p. 132.

109 CALLED THE TERMS: McDonald, *International Syndicated Loans*, pp. 42–43.

110 AT CHEAPER RATES: Ibid., p. 44.

112 THOSE FROZEN ASSETS: Ibid., p. 44.

112 GENERATIONS OF LAWYERS: Sampson, *The Money Lenders*, p. 146.

CHAPTER 6: *A Roving Commission*

PAGE

120 BY OUTSTANDING LOANS: This was told to me by the head of Bank Leumi le-Israel's international division during a trip to Tel Aviv in 1980. Since most banks—especially the bigger ones—are paranoiacally discreet about their loan portfolios in Israel, it is impossible to verify. But all other evidence seems to confirm it.

122 TO ARGENTINA: "Banking Takes a Beating," *Time*, December 3, 1984, p. 59, and S. C. Gwynne, "Can Bank of America Repossess Brazil?," *California*, November 1984, p. 111.

122 $350 BILLION TO AMERICAN BANKS: "Banking Takes a Beating," p. 59.

122 LOCATED IN MONEY CENTERS: "Bank Scoreboard," *Business Week*, April 19, 1984, p. 83.

123 $15 BILLION IN 1979: "World Debt Tables—1979," World Bank.

124 DEBT EVEN HEAVIER: "Inflation Gone Rampant," *Time*, July 28, 1980.

124 GROSS NATIONAL PRODUCT: David K. Shipler, "Inflation Besets Israel," *New York Times*, February 3, 1980.

124 INTO THE MILITARY: Ibid.

124 A MILLION DOLLARS A DAY: "World Debt in Crisis," *Wall Street Journal*, June 22, 1984, p. 31.

CHAPTER 7: *Trouble in Paradise*

PAGE

129 AND THE PHILIPPINES: *Cleveland Trust Annual Report, 1983.*

129 BY THE END OF 1984: Edwin A. Finn, Jr., "Many Regional Banks Reduce Foreign Loans, Raise Tough Problems," *Wall Street Journal,* November 19, 1984, p. 1, quote from Charles Hammel.

129 CLEVELAND TRUST AMONG THEM: Darrell Delamaide, *Debt Shock: The Full Story of the World Credit Crisis* (Garden City, N.Y.: Anchor/Doubleday, 1984), p. 74.

133 THROUGH THE DECADE: Anthony Spaeth, "Family's Struggle Mirrors Philippines' Plight," *Wall Street Journal,* August 7, 1984, p. 24.

135 MANILA BAY RECLAMATION PROJECT: Guy Sacerdoti, "Operation Cold Comfort," *Far Eastern Economic Review,* May 14, 1982, p. 87.

135 MORE THAN 4 TO 1: Guy Sacerdoti, "Shaken Foundations," *Far Eastern Economic Review,* October 15, 1982, pp. 88–89.

136 THE ORIENT TWO YEARS LATER: CDCP's crisis was reported in depth in the *Far Eastern Economic Review, Asian Wall Street Journal,* and in the Philippine press.

138 AND THE OTHER REGIONALS: Sacerdoti, "Operation Cold Comfort," and "Shaken Foundations."

139 "HISTORY OF THE PHILIPPINES": Guy Sacerdoti, "A Bailed Out Case," *Far Eastern Economic Review,* March 24, 1983, pp. 78–80.

140 TO 483 CREDITOR BANKS: Steve Lohr, "Manila Signs IMF Letter," *New York Times,* September 21, 1984, p. D-9.

141 THE BANKS' GROWING CONCERNS: "Manila in Need of Long Term Loans," *New York Times,* October 11, 1983.

141 44 PERCENT, OR $9.1 BILLION, WAS DUE: "Philippines Wins Delay in '83 Repayment," *New York Times,* October 15, 1983, p. 35.

141 TO FEED THE NATION: Lohr, "Manila Signs IMF Letter."

141 AND BY THE IMF: Anthony Spaeth and Cheah Cheng, "Philippines' Foreign Exchange Crisis May Ease by Fall," *Wall Street Journal,* June 29, 1984, p. 33.

141 EXCHANGE RESERVES BY $1.8 BILLION: "Marcos and the IMF," *Wall Street Journal,* editorial, August 24, 1984.

142 DECEMBER 31, 1983: *Bank of California Annual Report, 1983.*

143 THE PAST TWENTY YEARS: "Marcos and the IMF."

CHAPTER 8: *The $195-Million Burn*

PAGE

145 ALL AMERICAN BANK DEBT: Edwin A. Finn, Jr., "Many Regional Banks Reduce Foreign Loans, Raise Tough Problems," *Wall Street Journal,* November 19, 1984, p. 1.

145 HELD BY OHIO BANKS: Rick Reiff, "Banks Uneasy over Latin Loans," *Akron Beacon Journal,* June 4, 1984.

146 PRINCIPAL UNTIL 1984: Darrell Delamaide, *Debt Shock: The Full Story of the World Credit Crisis* (Garden City, N.Y.: Anchor/Doubleday, 1984), p. 109.

146 180-ODD REGIONAL BANKS: Finn, "Many Regional Banks."

PAGE

150 LEFT TO PAY DEBT: Larry A. Sjaastad, "Where the Latin American Loans Went," *Fortune*, November 26, 1984.

152 TO $17.4 BILLION: Delamaide, *Debt Shock*, p. 127.

153 OVER 100 PERCENT IN 1979: Norman Gall, "Games Bankers Play," *Forbes*, December 5, 1983.

153 AND HEALTH CARE: Ibid.

156 "ITS UGLY NAKEDNESS": Delamaide, *Debt Shock*, p. 99.

CHAPTER 9: *The Phony End of the Debt Crisis*

PAGE

159 HAMMEL HAD NO CONTROL: From *Cleveland Trust Annual Reports, 1983, 1984*.

159 FROM THE THIRD WORLD: Edwin A. Finn, Jr., "Many Regional Banks Reduce Foreign Loans, Raise Tough Problems," *Wall Street Journal*, November 19, 1984.

159 BY ANOTHER 10 PERCENT: Gary M. Levin, "Jarrett: Ameritrust Plan Will End Flat Profits," *Crain's Cleveland Business*, December 26, 1983.

160 $48.50 A SHARE: From *Cleveland Trust Annual Reports, 1983, 1984*.

161 TO ARGENTINA ALONE: "Internationalization of U.S. Banks Falters," *Wall Street Journal*, August 7, 1984.

161 CHEMICAL 193 PERCENT: Rick Reiff, "Banks Uneasy over Latin Loans," *Akron Beacon Journal*, June 4, 1984.

162 TO THE REGIONALS: Finn, "Many Regional Banks."

162 IN THIS CENTURY: S. C. Gwynne, "Can Bank of America Repossess Brazil?," *California*, November 1984, p. 108.

162 TO $336 BILLION: Charles E. Schumer and Alfred J. Watkins, "Faustian Finance," *New Republic*, May 11, 1985, p. 14.

163 $19 BILLION IN INTEREST: Ibid.

163 $38 BILLION IN INTEREST PAYMENTS: Ibid.

164 UP AGAINST THE WALL: Ibid.

165 OUT OF THE WOODS: "Nightly Business Report," National Public Radio, May 25, 1985.

165 "ON ITS COMMERCIAL INTEREST": Karin Lissakers, "Dateline Wall Street: Faustian Finance," *Foreign Policy*, Fall 1983, p. 160.

165 "AN EXTENDED AGREEMENT FROM IT": "Third World Lightning Rod," *Time*, July 2, 1984, p. 49.

165 QUOTA AT $19.2 BILLION: "How the IMF Works," *Great Decisions '84*, New York: Foreign Policy Association, p. 50.

166 U.S. TAX DOLLARS: Lissakers, "Dateline Wall Street."

166 TO AMORTIZE PRINCIPAL: Ibid.

166 A "FAUSTIAN BARGAIN": Schumer and Watkins, "Faustian Finance."

166 "LOOSE BANKING PRACTICES": Lissakers, "Dateline Wall Street."

166 "EARLIER ROUNDS OF INTEREST": Schumer and Watkins, "Faustian Finance."

168 MORE OF THE BURDEN: Finn, "Many Regional Banks."

168 EVEN AT $207 BILLION: Ibid.

169 TO DO THE SAME: Ibid.

BIBLIOGRAPHY

The following articles served as background on the international debt crisis:

"Austerity Straps Brazil." *Business Week,* October 17, 1983, p. 62.

"Banks on Brink." *Progressive,* April 1983, p. 12.

"Birth of Borrowers' Cartel." *Newsweek,* September 5, 1983, pp. 56–57.

"Crisis: World Deflation." *Forbes,* October 10, 1983, pp. 222–23.

"Deeper and Deeper in Debt [Argentina]." *Macleans,* October 17, 1983, p. 49.

"Do Not Pay $40 Billion, Go Directly to Jail [Argentina]." *Newsweek,* October 17, 1983, p. 38.

"Foreign Debt $400 Billion." *U.S. News and World Report,* December 20, 1982, p. 14.

"IMF Dilemma." *Business Week,* July 25, 1983, pp. 58–59.

"IMF Is Less and Less Able to Stop the Bleeding." *Business Week,* October 10, 1983, p. 28.

"IMF: Loony Lending." *National Review,* October 14, 1983, pp. 1, 260.

"Mexico." *National Review,* September 17, 1982, pp. 1, 173.

"Mexico Tightens Belt." *Time.* June 13, 1983, pp. 48–50.

"New Debt Crisis." *U.S. News and World Report,* July 4, 1983, pp. 49–50.

"Now Romania." *Business Week,* February 1, 1982, p. 63.

"Poland." *Forbes,* August 29, 1983, p. 31.

"Polish Bail-out." *Business Week,* February 15, 1982, pp. 42–43.

"Pulling the Economic Plug [Eastern Europe]." *National Review,* March 19, 1982, p. 276.

"Trap for Banks in Third World Bailout." *Business Week,* January 20, 1983, pp. 168–69.

"Why Brazil Scares Us." *Esquire,* October 1983, p. 12.

"World Debt Bomb." *U.S. News and World Report,* October 10, 1983, pp. 95–96.

"World of Shaky Debts." *Newsweek,* September 6, 1982, p. 62.

"Write Down Loans?" *Forbes,* May 9, 1983, pp. 57–60.

"Year of Default." *Progressive,* December 1982, pp. 11–12.

In addition, the following books provided useful information:

De Roover, Raymond. *The Rise and Decline of the Medici Bank: 1397–1494.* Cambridge, Mass.: Harvard University Press, 1963..

Donaldson, T. H. *International Lending by Commercial Banks.* New York: John Wiley and Sons, 1979.

Kindleberger, Charles P. *Manias, Panics, and Crashes: A History of Financial Crises.* New York: Basic Books, 1978.

Mayer, Martin. *The Bankers.* New York: Weybright and Talley, 1974.

For a complete list of books available from Penguin in the United States, write to Dept. DG, Penguin Books, 299 Murray Hill Parkway, East Rutherford, New Jersey 07073.

For a complete list of books available from Penguin in Canada, write to Penguin Books Canada Limited, 2801 John Street, Markham, Ontario L3R 1B4.